Ethiopianism:
The Forgotten
Movement

Ethiopianism: The Forgotten Movement

The Role of Ethiopianism in the Pan-African Movement in Britain 1892-1906

BY

Danny Thompson

EVOLVING CREATIVES
London (UK)

Ethiopianism:
The Forgotten Movement

Cover Design by Jeorge Asare-Djan. Contact: jeorge@hotmail.co.uk

ACKNOWLEDGEMENTS

Special thanks to my family for their unwavering love and support during this project.

Thanks to Professor Hakim Adi of Chichester University for his guidance, and to my fellow students for their support.

In gratitude to Tehuti and Seshat for spiritual guidance.

TABLE OF CONTENTS

INTRODUCTION

Imagine an international network of Black student activists and church ministers imbued with a radical zeal to challenge colonialism and restore African culture and pride. Imagine this network sharing ideas and creating Black Christian nationalist organisations.

Such a network did exist, and from it arose a movement. It was called Ethiopianism.

Ethiopianism was a global black Nationalist movement which reached its zenith in the late nineteenth and early twentieth centuries. Centred in an African Christian liberation ideology Its biblically inspired ideas travelled on an African revolutionary wave from the United States to Africa to the Caribbean and to Europe.

It inspired religious movements which built hundreds of radical churches across the U.S. Africa. and the Caribbean. It produced some of the most significant African theologists, and activists of the nineteenth century. It played a major part in the post-enslavement growth of the Afro-American intellectual class. It did this through the religious and educational institutions it built and the self-help economic activism it both preached and practised. In West Africa it fuelled the creation of an educated intelligentsia. In Southern, Western, and Central Africa it created revolutionary leadership instrumental in challenging Colonialism and Apartheid and spiritually fuelling the drive towards independence. In Britain it was the centre of gravity for a host of Pan-African organisations and activists.

This book came about as a result of research I conducted for my MRes at Chichester University in 2021 under the guidance of Professor Hakim Adi.

The aim of my research was to explore and analyse the role Ethiopianism played within the black nationalist movement centred in Britain during the period 1892 - 1906. This involved my researching the origins of the movement, its ideologies, its key players, and its global expressions and nuances. Ethiopianism reached its influential height in Africa and the Diaspora in the period 1880 - 1920. Towards the end of this period saw the rise of Pan-Africanism as a formalised global ideology. Many of the tenets of Ethiopianism can be seen in later Pan-African ideology hence its place as a

Figure 1. Congelese procession in Colwyn Bay, Wales. This recognises Britain's role in the evolution of Pan-African and related ideas.

fore-runner of it. The term 'Pan-African' came into usage around 1900. By the second and third Pan-African Congresses held in London in 1921 and 1923 respectively, it had become the globally recognised term adopted by African Liberation organisations in their liberation struggles.

CHAPTER ONE: WHAT WAS ETHIOPIANISM?

The nineteenth century saw an intensification and gradual transformation of European domination across Africa. This culminated in the Berlin Conference in 1884 where competing European States and the U.S. reached agreement on their ownership and territorial boundaries within the African continent.

The Berlin Conference symbolised the completion of a transition from the European enslavement system which European States were gradually forced to abolish during the mid-nineteenth century. And the establishment of the colonial system which secured their continued political, economic, social, and religious domination over Africans worldwide well into the twentieth century. The rise of Colonialism and Imperialism brought with it a rise in racist attitudes against Africans. This was a reversal of the English abolitionist liberal attitudes whose advocates had influenced the discourse on Africans in the first half of that century.

1896 saw the Ethiopian defeat of Italy's attempted invasion. This victory, culminating in the Battle of Adwa where Emperor Menelik II defeated the invading Italian army, became a rallying point and a beacon of hope for Africans worldwide. Menelik II invited Africans from the diaspora to return 'home' and receive education, training, and assist Africa's development. The Battle of Adwa was to have huge symbolic importance for generations to come. Despite this, Africans on the continent, and across the Diaspora; the U.S. Caribbean, Central and South America continued to be subject to various forms of colonisation, from the creation of the Apartheid system in South Africa to the plantation system in Jamaica to 'Jim Crow' segregation in the U.S. It is within this context that the tenets of Ethiopianism were developed and actioned by Africans globally.

Ethiopianism - The Scholars views

During the early to mid nineteenth century, Ethiopianism was birthed as an ideology in two distinct forms: as a religious movement, and in literary form. The term Ethiopianism is somewhat generic as it covers a range of ideas and strategies ranging from the strictly religious to the overtly Pan-African. For its

Figure 2. Newspaper cartoon of the Berlin Conference 1884 depicting European nations dividing up Africa for themselves.

core ideals I quote from by Charles Reavis Price in his book *Expressions of Ethiopianism in Jamaica.* In it he identifies these basic ideals:

Fundamental Ideals of Ethiopianism

1.   Blacks should name themselves and reject names given to them by whites.
2.   Whites are naturally aggressive and acquisitive.
3.   God in human form is black, and deliberately mis-portrayed as white.
4.   Blacks should direct their own religious and secular destinies.
5.   Ethiopia is the symbolic home of all Black people and the root of their cultural and historical legacies, especially for Christian Blacks.
6.   This connection gives Blacks a direct claim to Ancient civilisations and history.
7.   Ethiopia/Africa is the place to where Blacks should return and/or should develop through financial and political investment.
8.   God will intercede on behalf of Blacks against Whites.
9.   Those involved in slavery will be destroyed by God.
10.   Blacks are a noble race brought low by White oppression.

He also identifies three main factors for Ethiopianism to take place:
1.   White hegemony - over liberty, knowledge, and religion.
2.   A desire of Blacks for varying degrees of autonomy in economic and political affairs.

3.   A sense of injustice and moral wrong relating to Blacks enduring white injustices, especially slavery, colonialism and apartheid.

To this I would add English scholar George Shepperson's demographic observation that "Ethiopianism appears in Africa when there is a large Euro or European influenced ruling class, permanently resident, missionary education, and Euro churches predominantly protestant". This last observation helps us to understand why Ethiopianism never appeared in Britain or Europe in the form it had in the U.S. Africa, and the Caribbean. Britain, despite having a substantial African population stretching from Edinburgh in Scotland to Cardiff in Wales. And from Liverpool to London to Bristol in England. They did not have the physically segregated black communities where they could create independent black churches where Ethiopianism could develop. As we shall see this resulted in an intellectual collaboration and proselytizing of Ethiopianism but no direct organizing of the masses under the term.

Across Africa and the Diaspora Ethiopianist organisations and churches shared these basic beliefs to varying degrees, adapting them to their own particular circumstances. Some adopted a secular predominately economic and political interpretation and expression whilst others leaned towards a predominantly religious interpretation. Within the Ethiopianist discourse was reflected the wider liberation discourse and its inherent frictions and contradictions. Between those seeking radical or revolutionary solutions and those seeking accommodation within the colonial system. Some followed a strictly prophetic ideology of waiting for godly intervention whilst others followed a repatriation and reparation ideology that called for more direct action. Both involved teaching African people about their glorious history whilst encouraging them to reclaim it.

The Role of Ethiopia

In order to understand Ethiopianism and its evolution it is important to understand the mythology of Ethiopia in the nineteenth century and the impact of that mythology for Africans. The term 'Ethiopianism' relates both to the country Ethiopia, and to a Philosophical ideology of Black liberation, though not necessarily the two simultaneously. Historically the name Ethiopia has ancient origins and was once the name used by Europeans for all Africans and for the continent itself. The King James Bible written in 1611, an English translation from the earlier Hebrew & Greek version, emphasized the term 'Ethiopia' as a reference to Africans. Enslaved and colonized Africans, denied their indigenous spirituality and religious practices, were converted to Christianity via the King James Bible. They embraced the term 'Ethiopian' as

Figure 3. Ethiopian painting of the Battle of Adwa 1896 where Emperor Menelik II's armies defeated the invading Italian army.

self-defining. Biblically the Ethiopianism gospel is rooted in Psalm 68:31 "Princes shall come out of Egypt. Ethiopia shall stretch forth her hands unto God". This passage, particularly the second part was adopted by African Christians as a prophetic declaration of future liberation from European oppression as well as an assertion of African identity.

Ethiopia the country was also of significance in its position as unconquered by Europeans and it had its own Coptic Christian religion not subject to European Christianization. The Ethiopian Christian tradition has its roots in the ancient Nile Valley civilization which stretched from Uganda and Somalia in the south to Egypt in the north. Knowledge of this heritage was vital in keeping Africans of the eighteenth, nineteenth and twentieth centuries connected to a great Ancient African civilization. Leonard Barrett, in his book *The Rastafarians: Sounds of Cultural Dissonance* wrote:

> It was the vision of a golden past and the promise that Ethiopia should once more stretch forth its hands to God that revitalized the hope of an oppressed people. Ethiopia to the Blacks in the Diaspora was like Zion or Jerusalem to the Jews.

Bengt Sundkler, a writer on Ethiopianism in Africa echoes this observation,

The Ethiopian mythology projects the longings of the Africans to a Christian African nation under the 'Lion of Judah, King of Kings' and that its adherents sought out Mt. Zion 'City of the living God, heavenly Jerusalem.

J. Casely-Hayford the Ghanaian Ethiopianist crystalized these sentiments "An understanding of Christianity's roots in Ethiopia, which has never been colonized came to be recognized as a 'Metaphysical Black Heaven". Many Black churches and their related organizations adopted and adapted this Biblical prophecy. Nurtured in the proselytizing missionary nature of the Christianity they had been taught by Europeans they preached their own 'Black Heaven' version to the wider Black communities. This has led scholars on Ethiopianism such as French researcher Badra Lahouel to conclude "Ethiopianism is above all a religious movement". Whilst this may be true of its origins and earliest forms, to my mind it does not suffice as a complete definition of Ethiopianism. From the mid nineteenth century onwards, its activities moved beyond the religious into the political, and economic spectrum of African life. The ideology brought it into direct conflict with existing colonial systems. Ethiopianism gives us an example of the creativity of Africans under enslavement in their ability to take an ideology, Christianity, used by Europeans as a tool of subjugation and transform it into a tool of liberation. It also reflects the African practice of revolutionary spiritual leadership, whether through traditional spiritual practices or Christian practice.

Origins of Ethiopianism

The Ethiopianist church movement grew out of Africans rejection of a European missionary education and its inherent colonial values and policies. This allied to a need for an alternative African centred spirituality. Three important locations in the development of the ideology were the U.S.A. The African continent, and The Caribbean. Communalities they shared were that African populations in these locations were concentrated, segregated, and under the control of a European or European influenced ruling class. They were subject to a Christian Missionary education system.

Ethiopianism in the U.S.

In the U.S. the rise of churches such as the African Methodist Episcopal Church (AMEC) rejected this hypocrisy. Founded in 1787 in Philadelphia by Richard Allen, he was a member of the Free African Society, a mutual aid society he transformed into an African congregation. The AMEC was initially an umbrella organization for Black churches dissatisfied with the racial discrimination within the American church. It produced literature and preached

Figure 4. David
Walker, U.S. Author,
Activist. Considered
one of the founders of
the Ethiopianist
movement.

sermons critiquing Eurocentric Christianity. It educated its congregation on the
Black presence in the Bible. They seceded from their European religious
masters setting up their own church and preaching their own liturgy. They
adapted the missionary techniques they had been taught and created their own
missionaries who they sent out across the U.S. and into Africa with an
Ethiopianist doctrine described by Graham Duncan as "creating a corporate
African cultural identity through its heritage, a distinctive African spirituality,
Pan Africanism and autonomy". There were differences in the styles of
worship practised by U.S. 'Ethiopian' churches. The clearest examples of this
are the AMEC which practised a strict Christian liturgy and conservative style
of worship, and the AMEZ (Zionist) church which incorporated Traditional
African practices in its style of worship such as drums, dance, and traditional
healing practices. Within these U.S. examples can also be seen the impact of
class. The AMEC representing the growing Afro-American middle class whose
retention of African tradition could be described as a more intellectual pursuit.
Whilst the AMEZ, also with a middle-class leadership, would attract a more
'country folk' congregation whos' retention of African traditions was more
functional.

   Graham Duncan in his work *Ethiopianism in Pan-African Perspective 1880-
1920* presents his analysis of the development of Ethiopianism in the U.S. and
its relationship and impact on Africa. Beginning with the U.S. based 'Africa
for Africans' movement in the eighteenth century he places the development of
Ethiopianism alongside the development of African American consciousness
post emancipation and post reconstruction, particularly the rise of the African
American intellectual elite. An elite led by David Walker and Edward Blyden

who both made significant intellectual contributions to the ideology of Ethiopianism in the U.S. They helped birth Ethiopianism as a literary tradition in the U.S.

"Arise! Arise! Strike for your lives and liberties. Now is the day and hour". So wrote David Walker in his incendiary work *Appeal in Four Articles* written in 1829.Born in North Carolina in 1785 to a free Mother and enslaved Father, Walker experienced the full horror of enslavement in the southern states of the U.S. After travelling through the U.S., he settled in Boston where he became a leading abolitionist. Famed as a fiery public speaker against enslavement he teamed up with fellow abolitionist, Baptist minister Thomas Paul, and founded the U.S.' first African American newspaper 'Freedoms Journal' in 1828. As a member of the Massachusetts General Colored Association he organised meetings where he called for the political and organizational unity of the black community. A devout Christian he firmly believed that:

> oppressed people were called upon to act as well as pray … I verily believe that God has something in reserve for us, which when he shall have poured it out upon us, will repay us for all our suffering and misery.

One of the things that made Walker's book stand apart from other abolitionist literature of the period was that it was addressed specifically to Black people. It contained no appeals to white liberals or white liberalism. As well as informing Blacks of their glorious heritage and lessons to be learned from it, it critically examined the actions of the enslavers themselves. The range of topics dealt with ranged from an examination of Ancient Carthage and the Haitian revolution. How the huge potential of both events were eventually betrayed by disunity. He drew contemporary comparisons with the potential of African Americans and that potential being crippled by disunity. A disunity he identified as rooted in the deliberate efforts to keep Blacks ignorant of their history. He invited Blacks to use his Appeal to "go to work and enlighten our brethren", and declared:

> I advance it therefore to you, not as problematical but as an unshaken and ever immovable fact, that your full glory and happiness, as well as all other coloured people under Heaven, shall never be consummated, but with the entire emancipation of your enslaved brethren all over the world.

The Appeal examined "the hypocrisy and cruelty of America's 'enlightened white Christians". He claimed Blacks had a divine right and duty to fight back without mercy". He attacked ex- President Thomas Jefferson's declaration that," Blacks were inferior to Whites in the endowments of both body and mind". He attacked this philosophy of Scientific racism as having the effect of

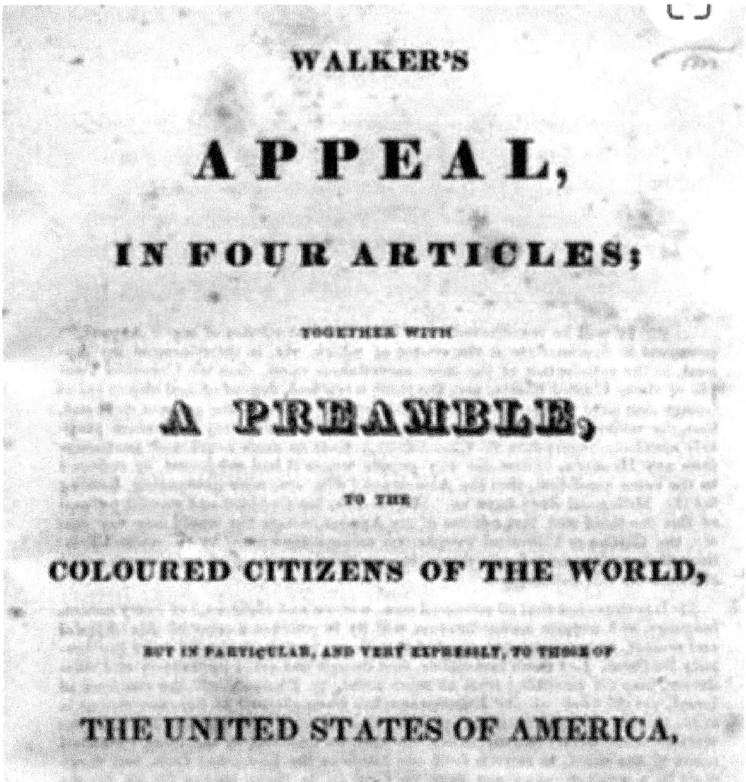

WALKER'S

APPEAL,

IN FOUR ARTICLES;

TOGETHER WITH

A PREAMBLE,

TO THE

COLOURED CITIZENS OF THE WORLD,

BUT IN PARTICULAR, AND VERY EXPRESSLY, TO THOSE OF

THE UNITED STATES OF AMERICA,

WRITTEN IN BOSTON, STATE OF MASSACHUSETTS,
SEPTEMBER 28, 1829.

THIRD AND LAST EDITION,
WITH ADDITIONAL NOTES, CORRECTIONS, &c.

Boston:
REVISED AND PUBLISHED BY DAVID WALKER.

1830.

Figure 5. Cover page of David Walker's *Appeal in Four Articles* originally written in 1829.

"defamation and the crippling of black's character and intellect" and of "casting upon African Americans the stigma of inherent inferiority and degradation". He advocated Black self-reliance and moral responsibility for liberating themselves. Faith that the kingdom of God can be inaugurated on earth, the special relationship between Blacks and God and the divine mandate.

Within this breakdown of Walker's beliefs, we see the elements of 'Ethiopianism' in the U.S. The divine mandate, moral high ground, black self-reliance, and the creation of a 'kingdom of God' I.e. A separate land for Gods' 'black' children. Walker further argued "If whites sought to kill blacks, or if blacks decided to rise up and slay whites, then 'kill or be killed". *Appeal in Four Articles* was considered so radical and threatening to the white power structure that upon its publication the state of Georgia immediately passed a bill banning any further publication and distribution. Possession of the book was also banned upon penalty of death. The law forbidden the teaching of reading and writing to Blacks was also strengthened. This ban was extended to the States of Virginia and North Carolina and a $1000 bounty placed on its author. As was the case with much abolitionist literature of the time African Americans found ingenious ways to distribute Walkers' work. Copies were stitched into the lining of clothing or smuggled aboard merchant ships. Secret sessions were organised where it was read and discussed. The impact on African Americans of Walkers' *Appeal in Four Articles* was so huge it went through three editions even if they had to read it clandestinely.

Edward Blyden who came to prominence in late 19th century took a historical and theological approach in his work *Christianity, Islam, and the Negro Race,* written in 1887. He'd already established a reputation as an educationalist through his monthly journal *The Ethiopian* founded in 1872. The journal focused on educational matters for African Americans. In his book he attacked European Christianity and its white supremacist ideals, and suggested Islam as having more potential for blacks to achieve. He acknowledged the oppressive nature of both religions on Black people but argued Islam was a more meritocratic system and therefore offered more potential for Blacks to improve themselves. He encouraged blacks to study their African heritage.

In his analysis of the recent emancipation of Africans in the U.S. was that it shouldn't be seen as an isolated event but within the context of events leading to the regeneration of Africa. He raised the question of 'Emancipation, what next?' His proposed answer was to support the growing Exodus Associations facilitating the return of African Americans to Africa. He noted and predicted the rise of European interest in the African continent and encouraged African Americans to do the same.

The European interest included the growing study of the African psychology. In response he claimed Europeans as being incapable of comprehending the

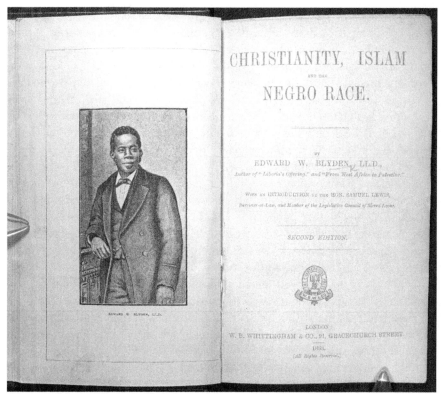

Figure 6. Edward Blyden's *Christianity, Islam, and the Negro Race*, originally 1887, this is the second edition.

African mind due to their own White supremacist psychology. Blyden's own psychological analysis of Europeans grouped them into four classes: The philanthropic Liberal. The redneck hater. The indifferent. Those who treat Blacks as they would others (the smallest group). He concluded all are harmful to the Black race.

Blyden was a member of the American Colonisation Society (ACS), a controversial U.S. government supported body dedicated to black emigration to Africa, particularly Liberia in West Africa. It was considered controversial due to its governmental backing. Many Blacks argued the U.S. government had no interest in the welfare of African Americans and the ACS was a method to rid itself of its 'White mans burden'. Blyden himself emigrated to Liberia in the 1890s. He described Liberia as "a place where Africans could mature… where white is dethroned and black takes its proper position" Blyden conceived the idea of a West African Church and encouraged African Americans to return to their roots in Africa and to their cultural and religious heritage under the slogan of unity: 'Africa for Africans'.

Blyden's works were very influential among the new African American intellectual elites. They embraced it as it gave them an alternative empowering vision of the future, a vision intrinsically tied to Africa. He was also very influential among West African nationalists. J. Casely-Hayford, Ghanaian Ethiopianist, in his seminal work *Ethiopia Unbound* wrote a comparison of Booker T. Washington, W.E.B. Dubois, and Blyden. He concluded

> Edward Wilmot Blyden has sought for a quarter of a century to reveal the African unto himself. To fix his attention upon original ideas and conceptions as to his place in the economy of the world. To point out to him his work as a race among the races of men. Lastly, and most important of all, to lead him back unto self-respect. He has been the voice of one crying in the wilderness … he is the greatest living exponent of the true African nationality and manhood.

The work of these two giants added to the works of other leading Ethiopianists in the U.S. Henry Highland Garnett, Martin Delaney, Alexander Crummell created an intellectual body of work which took Ethiopianism beyond the emotive romantic and providential niche into a Black Nationalist program albeit still rooted in a vision of a 'true' Christianity.

From the late eighteenth century there were 'Exodus Associations' and 'Emigration Societies' in the U.S. dedicated to repatriation in Africa. Though small in number they represented an acknowledgement of Africa as their homeland, a desire to return, and a growing African American consciousness. By the mid nineteenth century independent African American churches were promoting emigration, the missionary imperative, and educational exchanges with Africans. Africans travelled to the U.S. to receive an Ethiopianist education from African American church colleges before returning to Africa as missionaries. For these young African students attending these church colleges brought them into contact with students from other African nations. This contact promoted a 'Pan-African' type unity as they were able to recognise the similarities between their national struggles.

The hub of this work was without doubt the African Methodist Episcopal Church (AMEC) founded in 1815, of which he says, "over the next century the AMEC became the body around which African separation grouped itself". The AMEC like the AICs in Africa separated from the white American led Methodist church and proselytized the 'divine mandate' expressed by Walker and Blyden. The AMEC reflected the nature of African American churches which were always more than simply places of worship. As one of the few places where African Americans could congregate without direct European control they served as a community resource beyond just spiritual matters. As such they were a hub for all manner of African American discourse including ideas around separatism and emigration. Ethiopianism gave these ideas a

Figure 7. Reverend Richard Allen, founder of the African Methodist Episcopal Church in the U.S.

spiritual imperative and reinforced this notion of 'exodus' as a divine imperative. Two prominent leaders of the AMEC were its founder Richard Allen and its most influential leader Bishop Henry McNeal Turner. Richard Allen who was a member of the 'Africa for Africans' movement. Duncan describes his ethos as "expressing a corporate African cultural identity through its heritage, a distinctive African spirituality, Pan-Africanism ..." The AMEC reached its heights of influence and activism through the leadership of Bishop Henry McNeal Turner who became head in 1880. Over the next twenty years he raised the profile of the AMEC in Africa through sending Ethiopianist missionaries there, receiving students from Africa, and organising emigrations of African Americans to Southern and Western Africa. The AMEC was particularly influential in South Africa where African Americans were seen as aspirational figures. Bishop McNeal visited and toured South Africa in 1893, 1895, and 1898, where he was treated as a heroic figure. The AMEC's exploits in South Africa were not without controversy as there were accusations made of U.S. arrogance and patronising attitudes to the indigenous population.

The literary expressions of Ethiopianism in the U.S. during the nineteenth century offered a wide range of interpretations of the providential design. U.S. author Robert Alexander Young wrote the incendiary text *The Ethiopian Manifesto* in 1829. A strictly religious text he prophesised the coming of a Black Messiah. He wrote

> ... surely hath the cries of the Black, a most persecuted people, scended to my throne the craved my mercy; now behold! I will stretch forth my hand and gather them to the palm, that they may become unto me a people, and I unto them a God... Harken, therefore, oh Slaveholder, thou task inflicter against the rights of men, the day is at hand ...

Young claimed, "a universal freedom to every son and daughter descended from the Black God". He wrote that the messiah would be, paradoxically, a white man "bearing in himself the semblance of his former race, born of a black woman". The Messiah would have "two middle toes on each of his feet [that] would be webbed and bearded". "Ethiopians would pledge loyalty to this man and join in attacking every slaveholder. Their attack would unleash a time when poverty would appear a blessing (for Europeans) as Africans reclaimed their birthright and deliverance from wordly evil".

Despite its bizarre description of the Messiah, *The Ethiopianist Manifesto* and its message of a Messiah led revolution against whites became a hugely influential text in New York and the Northeastern coast.

Alongside these theological literary expressions of Ethiopianism was a body of poetic and fictional works expressing Ethiopianist ideas rooted in the vision of a rising Africa and declining West. W.E.B. Dubois, the great African American scholar and writer, wrote several poems and short stories exploring these themes. Francis Ellen Watkins Harper, a great African American writer wrote a celebrated poem *Ethiopia*. Paul laurence Dunbar wrote another *Ode to Ethiopia*. Alexander Crummell, a pioneering African American author, minister, nationalist, and activist, wrote extensively on Black nationalism in the mid nineteenth century. His sermons espoused an Ethiopianist doctrine.

Ethiopianism in Africa

In Africa, a similar rejection of European Missionary education took place during the mid to late nineteenth century resulting in the rise of African

Figure 8. Reverend H.M. Turner. Leader of the AMEC. Under his leadership it grew in influence in the U.S. and Africa.

REV. H. M. TURNER, CHAPLAIN FIRST UNITED STATES COLORED REGIMENT.

Independent Churches (A.I.C.). And the Independent Bantu Church Movement based predominantly in Southern Africa. By the beginning of the C20th they had grown to number hundreds of independent African Christian Churches all preaching an Ethiopianist doctrine or a near enough variation. B. Lahouel in his work *Ethiopianism and African Nationalism in South Africa before 1937* states "African churches ... a result of consciousness of European oppression both material and spiritual and the need for a theology to occupy political, social, and economic spaces". This need for a spirituality that reflected their reality and empowered them to change that reality was a key element in the rise of Ethiopianism.

B. Lahouel concludes "Ethiopianism was above all a religious movement.". In his analysis he highlights the problem of applying the term generically to all African churches.

> Yet if the Africans were eager to feel at home by retaining their personality, they simultaneously refused to give up their Christian faith. The two broad types of African churches Ethiopian and Zionist, both constituted emanations of African aspirations but they did not call Christian faith into question.

Lahouel is correct in his analysis of Ethiopianism as primarily a religious movement. But his separation of Ethiopian and Zionist churches are differences of form and practice not of goals. Both represented expressions of aspiration for liberation within a colonial context. Where some aspired within the colonial framework and others outside of it. Historian Kalu affirms that:

> Ethiopianism laid the foundations for modern forms of African nationalism whether in the political or ecclesiastical realm and initiated the current debates on inculturation and vernacularisation in African theology. They voice a new form of Christianity in Africa.

Lahouel explores the notion of African Christianity itself and its tension between retention of traditional African religions and adoption of the 'new' Christian religion, identifying efforts on the part of Ethiopianists to combine both. These attempts at a synthesis of the traditional and the new characterise the variations of practice within the umbrella of the term.

Some scholars presented Ethiopianism as solely a response to missionary education whilst others claimed it as part of a wider reaction to racial discrimination. Lahouel details the African reaction to missionary education and its inherent colour bar using examples from Lovedale and Healdtown, the two largest and most influential missionary schools in Southern Africa in the late nineteenth century, responsible for training Africans in Christian Theology and ordaining them into priesthood. These two colleges offered Africans the contradiction of receiving the highest levels of education then available to Africans whilst enforcing colonial and racist barriers to their advancement within the church and in wider society. African Christian activists such as Nehemiah Tile, Mangena Mokone, Lucas Zungu, all graduates from Lovedale and Healdtown left the Methodist church complaining of racial discrimination and theological hypocrisy and formed their own Ethiopianist churches. Lahouel explores the notion of African Christianity itself and its tension between retention of traditional African religions and adoption of the 'new' Christian religion, identifying efforts on the part of Ethiopianists to combine both. He explores the social and economic aspects of Ethiopianism in the context of the creation of the colonial apartheid system taking place during this period. For example: the reaction of African independent churches to the 1913 'Natives Land Act' which denied Africans the right to buy land in designated 'white areas', a legal foundation of the emerging Apartheid system. The Ethiopianist churches were at the forefront of the resistance against the act. In his final analysis he repeats his assertion of Ethiopianisim being above all, a religious movement fuelled by disillusionment with European led churches. But he expands this by saying it was a disillusionment which naturally led to a dialectical relationship between Ethiopianism and Nationalism.

Figure 9. An Independent South African church, fusing Christian and Traditional African spiritual beliefs.

According to Ethiopian scholar Getawachu Metaferia Ethiopianism gave its followers "a psychological confidence builder and a ray of hope to look forward to". This need to separate from European led churches and establish a new empowering identity is further demonstrated by the fact that whenever Black churches seceded, they named their churches African, or Abyssinian, or Ethiopian thus strengthening their connection to their African heritage.

Graham Duncan in his work *Ethiopianism in Pan African Perspective 1880-1920* presents a broader and I would argue a deeper exploration of Ethiopianism. "Ethiopianism became a generic term to describe a whole range of the black mans' efforts to improve his religious, educational, and political status in society". He presents it as a precursor to Pan-African nationalism. "Political awareness among the mass of the African population expressed itself in a religious form known as Ethiopianism." He begins the African history of Ethiopianism during the eighteenth century citing Kimpa Vita, a Congolese Freedom fighter and spiritual leader who adapted the Christianity forced upon her by the Portuguese into an African liberation theology. She preached Jesus and his disciples were African, Congo was the Garden of Eden, and heaven was reserved solely for Africans. She died in 1706 aged twenty-two. Duncan cites this as an early example of Ethiopianism even though it was not reliant on strictly Ethiopic Biblical references. It still however provides an early example of how Africans were reinterpreting the Eurocentric bible into a liberating text. Duncan traces the development of African Ethiopianism as a revolutionary impetus and draws a direct lineage from Kimpa Vita to the anti-colonial rebellions of Maitsope Makheto, Hendrik Witboi, Enoch Magijima, and John Chilembwe in Southern and Central Africa in the late nineteenth and early twentieth centuries. He places Ethiopianism firmly as part of the AIC movement as they had much in common "a response to colonialism, imperialism, and the missionary movement."

Duncan is one of the few scholars to document the influence of Ethiopianism in East Africa where the Anglican church was the dominant denomination. In the early twentieth century a combination of Garveyite Pan-Africanism and Southern African influenced Ethiopianism gave rise to independent African churches such as the African Orthodox church in Uganda and Kenya numbering approximately 10,000 members. He's also one of the few scholars to mention the role of women in these missionary initiatives.

> In Zambia, Alice Lenshina Mulenga's prophetic Lumpa Church may be described as a prophetic and Ethiopian-type church ... The Bible and the sacrament of Holy Communion were jettisoned while traditional practices were developed, eg. dance and polygamy.

This gives us a good example of the variations of Ethiopianism practiced in Africa. A hybrid of Christian doctrine and traditional practice.

Duncan writes on Ethiopianisms' relationship with the Pan-African movement and the nature of that influence.

> Ethiopianism laid the foundations of modern forms of African Nationalism whether in political or ecclesiastical realm ... The reason for the founding of the black church was missiological... they were formulators of the concept of Pan-Africanism.

Another scholar who covers similar territory to Duncan and Lahouel is George Shepperson in his work *Ethiopianism and African Nationalism* written in 1953. There are areas where he differs is in his definition and analysis of Ethiopianism. According to Shepperson there were two types; Those churches which were "secessionist from mainstream Wesleyn, Baptist, and Free churches. These churches associated themselves with U.S. Negro churches". And "Apocalyptic new churches, with origins in missionary efforts of white and black" He considers the first type as the correct application of the term. The second type he says had the label applied to them. The difference between Ethiopianism in West Africa and South Africa he describes thus "West African Nationalists initially used the term and thus it became a more generic term than specifically ecclesiastical. When they did use the term, they referred only to Africans, not to African Americans. This 'secular' use of the term in West

**Figure 10. Alice
Lenshina Mulenga.
Founder of the Lumpa
Church in Zambia.**

Africa was transported to Britain by West African students and intellectuals at the turn of the twentieth century. Duncan identifies twentieth century offshoots of the Ethiopianist churches in South Africa such as the Independent Bantu Church movement and the Christian Catholic Apostolic Church (CCAC) in Zion. These were considered dangerous by Europeans especially the CCAC which was run along the lines of a secret society.

A strength of Duncan's work is his connecting of Ethiopianism to political protest in Africa. His work on John Chilembwe, heavily influenced by Ethiopianism, who led a Native uprising in Nyasaland in the Congo in 1915 can be considered a template for Ethiopianist activism. African born Chilembwe travelled to the U.S. with John Booth, a radical English missionary who founded missions in Central Africa where he disseminated anti-colonial material and was eventually deported by the Colonial office. Whilst in the U.S. Chilembwe came under the influence of the American Negro Baptist Seminary where he was trained. Upon returning to Nyasaland, he headed the Providence Industrial Mission which became a focus for separatism. He personally led a rebellion which was forcibly put down by colonial forces, but which took on symbolic importance for Africans. Duncan identifies the late nineteenth and early twentieth centuries as the zenith of Ethiopianism as a movement in which "religion and politics reinforced each other in revolutionary ends." After this period Ethiopianism fades as political Pan-Africanism rose. What distinguishes Shepperson's work from others is his demographic analysis that

> True Ethiopianism appears in those parts of Africa in which there is a large European or European influenced ruling class … permanently resident and providing a missionary education.

He uses this analysis to assess why what he calls Ethiopianism had a stronger hold in Southern Africa than in Western Africa. And though he recognises the influence of African American Ethiopianism on Africa he argues "If no American Negro had set foot in Africa Ethiopianism would have taken the same course". This perspective is understandable taking into account his analysis of the conditions for Ethiopianism to take root. But it's undermined by the fact that those same demographic conditions existed in the southern states of the U.S. where Ethiopianism had its stronghold. Also, the missionary proselytising ethos of Ethiopianism was always going to result in collaboration between Africans on different continents. Duncan's work is very useful to my analysis of Ethiopianism in Britain as the Black British population did not have the demographic density of the U.S or Africa either in population or independent black churches.

Ethiopianism in the Caribbean

Together the scholars, intellectuals and their works mentioned above represent a reliable core body of research regarding African and African American Ethiopianism. Though some of its major figures, Edward Blyden for instance, had Caribbean origin, none of the above-mentioned scholars investigates Ethiopianism in the diaspora outside of the U.S. More recent work that has been done in this area includes Charles Reaves Price *'Cleave to the Black':* *Expressions of Ethiopianism in Jamaica,* published in 2003. He places Ethiopianism roots in an "understanding of Christianity's roots in Ethiopia, which has never been colonized." He traces the historical and theological lineage of Ethiopianism in Jamaica beginning with the arrival of Ethiopianists

Figure 11. George Lisle. U.S. Founder of the first 'Ethiopian Baptist Church' in Jamaica 1784.

such as George Lisle from the U.S. in 1784 who built the first 'Ethiopian Baptist Church' in Jamaica. Preaching that slavery was a sin and as Christians blacks had a moral duty not to submit to it, he was eventually charged with sedition. Moses Baker, another African American preacher arrived in Jamaica at the same time and worked alongside Lisle. Baker built the second black church in Jamaica in 1791.

Together they built a school for free and enslaved blacks and are credited with starting the Jamaica's Native Baptist Church tradition which was to have a strong tradition of radicalism on the island. The proliferation of European led churches in Jamaica and the rebellious retention of African traditions crystalized in the Morant Bay rebellion of 1865 led by Baptist Preacher Paul Bogle. A radical preacher he led a protest against social conditions which turned into a full-scale uprising lasting three days. His rallying cry was "Cleave to the black, kill all the white men and the black men that would join them" Though eventually put down and Bogle himself killed the rebellion became a unifying nationalist event which entered Jamaica folklore. Alexander Bedward, a self-styled radical preacher instructed his many followers, known as Bedwardites, that the British colonial government had oppressed them. He preached an apocalyptic Ethiopianism which predicted an oncoming confrontation between blacks and whites where blacks would emerge victorious.

> The present social order is doomed to destruction ... destined to be overthrown by a cataclysmic upheaval to society in the near future ... facilitated by blacks who would benefit from it.

He cited Bogle's Morant Bay rebellion as an inspiration. His followers were from the illiterate peasantry and his church had branches across Jamaica and in Cuba. His sermons of fiery deliverance resonated with the rising nationalistic sentiment in Jamaica. It also brought him into repeated conflict with the authorities and after many clashes he was eventually arrested and consigned to a mental asylum where he died in 1930. By this time the Rastafari religion was coming into existence in Jamaica and many of Bedwards followers took up his prophetic apocalyptic message and brought it into the religion. Paul Bogle's rallying cry was refined by early Rastafarians as "Death to all white and black oppressors". Moving forward the apocalyptic Ethiopianism of Bedward, Rastafari spoke of 'Babylon falling'. Babylon being a biblical symbol of sin and oppression. It's worth putting into context that from mid-nineteenth century to mid-twentieth century Jamaica had a strong tradition of radical preachers travelling from parish to parish delivering subversive and racial religious beliefs, most rooted in Ethiopianist biblical interpretations. Ethiopianism in this nineteenth century form led to the rise of Marcus Garvey and his brand of Pan-Africanism. Garvey's ideology contained strong elements of Ethiopianism. For example: his belief that "God must be seen through Ethiopian spectacles" and his supposed prophecy of an African King bringing redemption. This fits in well with the Ethiopianist idea of divine mandate and divine providence. An idea built on by Rastafarians who cite the crowning of Emperor Haile Selassie in 1930 as proof. Price's work is a very coherent model of Ethiopianism adapted to the particulars of its location and cultural context, in this case Jamaica. Price's work serves as a possible template for a similar investigation in other locations in the diaspora. It also reinforces Shepperson's assertion of the demographic conditions needed for Ethiopianism to flourish.

More Scholars views

Hakim Adi has produced a substantive body of work that addresses the nature of Pan-Africanism in Britain and the elements of Ethiopianism within it. In *Pan-Africanism and West African Nationalism in Britain* he advances the argument that Ethiopianism in West Africa expressed itself as a form of Nationalism. He argues its spread through West African students and organisations such as the Ethiopian Progressive Association, which had

Figure 12. Alexander Bedward. Radical Jamaican Pastor. He preached an Ethiopianist doctrine and had followers across the Caribbean.

branches in London and Liverpool, the Ethiopian Association in Edinburgh. The 'African Association' led by Henry Sylvester Williams was a late 19th century proponent of Ethiopianism containing African and Caribbean students and activists. His work focuses on the impact of African students in Britain at the turn of the 20th century and their impact on black activism in Britain. Extensive research has been done on The West African Medical Students Association and the West African Student Union (WASU). Though WASU came to prominence after 1920 its ideological roots can be traced earlier. West African activists in Britain such as Bandele Omoniyi made substantial contributions to British activism. His book *A Defence of the Ethiopianism Movement* in 1908, is an important addition to the literature of Ethiopianism. Adi draws a lineage of African activism in Britain from 18th and 19th century figures Olaudah Equiano and Ottobah Cugoano and their involvement in the abolitionist group 'Sons of Africa', to West African activist James Africanus Horton. In his book *Pan-Africanism - A History* 2018, he charts the history of Pan-Africanism as far back as the Haitian revolution 1791 and states 1872 as the birthdate of Ethiopianism in Africa when a number of churches in Lesotho seceded from French missions.

Another author in this subject area whose work I have drawn on is Marika Sherwood. Her essays *Origins of Pan-Africanism* are extensively researched and draw together different strands of Pan-Africanism. The African

Association, the first Pan-African Conference held in London in 1900, and a multitude of Caribbean activists passing through Britain including Henry Sylvester Williams and Edward Blyden.

Despite the differences in interpretation and application of the term, Ethiopianism can be defined thus: A black Christian Nationalist global movement of Africans who believed they had a divine mandate to take control of their own destinies. They would achieve this through education - in African history and the new sciences. Through organisation - of Africans for Africa. Through proselytising their message to the masses as well as to the ruling classes.

Ethiopianism gave form to a set of ideas that would later be called Pan-Africanism. The strategies used in attacking the colonial/imperialism structures and the ideologies that supported them laid the foundation for future Pan-Africanist activism. In many aspects there is no clear difference between the two. Where Ethiopianism ends and Pan-Africanism begins can only be clearly identified through usage of the terminology. At the beginning of the twentieth century many organisations and individuals used the term Ethiopianism. During the second decade of that century the term Pan-African came into common usage.

For the purposes of this paper, it's important to understand what, if anything, differentiates Ethiopianism and Pan-Africanism. Nigerian scholar Olisanwuche Esedebe *Pan-Africanism: The idea and Movement 1776-1991* argues:

> an accurate definition [of Pan-Africanism]... is by no means easy to formulate ... it's major components are: Africa as the homeland of Africans and persons of African origin. Solidarity among people of African descent. Belief in a distinct African personality. Rehabilitation of Africa's past, and pride in African culture. Africa for Africans in church and state. the hope for a united and glorious future Africa.

So in essence the overriding difference would be Ethiopianisms' desire for an African Christian Nation, though this too should be seen in the context of a vehicle to an independent Nation state. The consistent rejection of Eurocentric Christianity and adoption of an African centred 'true' Christianity is clear evidence of this.

CHAPTER TWO: BLACK PEOPLE IN BRITAIN 1890S

If you were a visitor to Britain in 1893, what would you see? You would see the most advanced industrial nation in the Western world celebrating the zenith of its Victorian power. The British Empire, the largest in the world and still gaining in power and territory through colonial expansion. If you stayed until 1900 you would witness the death of Queen Victoria and the birth of the Edwardian era. An age that solidified imperialist and colonialist conquest and expansion, which fuelled Britain's industrial revolution, and reinforced the attitudes that justified and drove its expansion. But what of Africans in Britain at this time. Who and where were they?

They were mature students, of whom most came to study with the intention of returning to their homelands once qualified. These students were often the progeny of African Royalty and wealthy Merchants under colonial rule. Others came via Missionary schools. Their studies included art, medicine, law, engineering, commerce, languages (notably Greek and Latin, necessary for undergraduate law students), French, and various apprenticeships in practical subjects. Whilst their residence gave them access to an elite English higher education it also brought them face to face with racism in the education system, in employment, and socially. Restrictions were placed not just on their employment in Britain but also on their employment in their colonised homelands, despite having gained qualifications in Britain.

They were Sailors, merchant and Royal Navy, mostly in temporary accommodation, though some had settled, whilst seeking work on ships visiting Britain's ports. By 1900 the city of Cardiff in Wales had the largest foreign-born population outside of London. The majority were seamen who'd been discarded once their ships had docked, and the shipping companies had no more use for them. They were cast out into a life of destitution. In 1910 a Parliamentary inquiry: 'The Committee on Distressed Colonial and Indian Subjects' reported that three in five distressed Blacks were seafaring men. A quarter were student adventurers. The Colonial Office repatriated some unemployed seamen, but in the case of the West Indians the authorities in the colonially ruled Islands they came from refused to let go back. According to the inquiry some of the destitute were West Indians who came to Britain to

Figure 13. Newspaper advert promoting the Great Exhibition in London 1852.

work as butlers and maids. Many had been forced to leave their employers due to ill treatment.

As well as Doctors and other medically trained staff there were entertainers, actors, composers, musicians, singers, dancers, mainly from the U.S. but also the Caribbean. If sport was your interest, you could go to a boxing match and place a bet on the African boxer to win. Or visit a North London stadium and watch a black professional footballer playing for one of the country's biggest teams. If in London at the Houses of Parliament or in Whitehall, you would come across diplomatic delegates from African colonies seeking an audience with the relevant political or religious organisations. If you were in Croydon, South London you would see West Africans out and about in traditional dress. In short, the last decade of the nineteenth century saw Africans from all corners of the British empire came to Britain for reasons of employment, education, or to petition the government and colonial offices on behalf of their homelands. By some accounts there was also a small Edwardian Black middle class dating back to the Victorian era. The presence of Africans in Britain stretched from Glasgow, Dundee, and Aberdeen in Scotland, to Wrexham, Cardiff, and Colwyn Bay in Wales. To Dublin, Belfast, Newry, Cork, Ennis, and Formay in Ireland. To the Jersey Isles off the southern coast of England. To Liverpool, Manchester, Lincoln, York, Bournemouth, Leeds, Harrogate, Bradford, Beverley, Hull, Scarborough, Brighton, Crawley, Rye. Grimsby, and Wigan. In rural areas such as Hampshire, Wiltshire, Cornwall, the Lake District, and St.

Figure 14. Postcard showing reconstruction of a Dahomey Village in White City, London 1909. The 'Villagers' were all actors.

Figure 15. Advertisement for Clico (Kliko), the Wild Dancing Bushman. 1899 Protestors had his show closed down for its dehumanizing portrayal of Africans.

Albans. In the capital London they were in the Central London, Acton, Edgware, Croydon.

The attitude of the majority working and middle-class population towards their colonial subjects was dictated by the colonialist propaganda of the time. Africans were seen as savages with little or no culture of worth. Cannibalism, massacre and torture were all attributed to Africans and Africa. Enslavement and Colonialism were projected as necessary 'civilising' projects for the benefit of Africans. Africans in Britain carried a novelty status, wrapped in superstitions and myths. A popular children's game of the period, 'Touch a N***er for Luck' best demonstrates the common view. A game white children played whenever an African appeared on the streets. Part social curiosity, part superstition. Britain's attitude can also be seen through their hugely popular exhibitions featuring these curious and exotic subjects. In this grand age of empire Britain was top dog among European nations and took every opportunity to display its wealth and influence.

These ostentatious displays began in 1851 with the Great Exhibition in Crystal Palace continued well into the Edwardian era with the Franco-British exhibition in 1908. There were permanent exhibitions in White City, London in 1909. These exhibitions were designed to show the British public the trappings of an empire built in their name. They often featured a display of African village life depicting the neo-savage natives to whom the British had brought civilisation. They featured Somalians, South Africans, Congolese. These village recreations featured adults and children in cages or large enclosed spaces where the public could view them. 'Savage South Africa', in London 1899, was a re-enactment of the conquests of Cecil Rhodes in the region. 'Klikko the Wild Dancing Bushman', London 1912. Klikko, a South African. His act was so humiliating that despite it being within the law it was protested by the Aborigines Protection Society. An English Society dedicated to ensuring the health the sovereign, legal, religious rights of indigenous peoples.

In 1905 The band of the West India Regiment consisting of forty members played at the Crystal Palace exhibition centre for several weeks, to a total audience numbering nine hundred thousand. In 1904 in the City of Bradford Exhibition where 'the most interesting black race in the world' was displayed. Somalian men, women, and children lived in a mock Somalian village carrying out traditional tasks. So popular was this exhibition that a side-trade grew in postcards of the village. They toured their 'village' in Edinburgh and in London. They were forced to protest outside Bradford Town Hall at their treatment, not only their living conditions but also their lack of wages. For the truth was they were actors. 1908 the Senegalese 'village' exhibited at the Franco-British Exhibition numbered over a hundred members and was

Figure 16. S.J. Celestine Edwards. Editor of *Lux & Fraternity* newspapers. Author of *Hard Truth*.

considered the most successful of all the villages on display. Like most of these exhibitions the 'villagers' were mostly actors. A fact that was kept from its audiences.

Another curiosity seen on the streets in the high offices of London were the visits of African Royalty, often at the invitation of the colonial office and powerful merchants with economic ties to Africa. In public they were accorded the pomp and status of Royalty. Behind the diplomatic niceties were serious discussions and petitions concerning the brutal colonial expansions being attempted in their home nations. King Lewanika, leader of the Barotse nation of Southern Africa visited Britain in 1902. Ostensibly to attend the coronation of King Edward but spent most of his time in London in meetings with the colonial office where he protested Cecil Rhodes establishment of Rhodesia and attempts at expansion had encroached on their lands.

The end of the nineteenth and beginning of the twentieth centuries saw a rise in the urbanisation of Britain prompted by the rise in industrialism and the need to house workers in these growing industrial centres. During this period Britain also re-imagined its' vision of itself. Projecting itself as a beacon of Christian civilisation with a mandate to bestow its gifts of civilisation on its lesser advanced colonial subjects. This was in fact a resurgence of an idea projected earlier in that century. The abolition of slavery in British colonies in 1834 was the zenith for its anti-slavery and abolitionist movements. Since that date the advocates and supporters of enslavement and colonialism had regrouped proselytising the 'Savage Natives' narrative and won the day. They promoted the doctrine of 'Commerce and Christianity'. First espoused by English missionary explorer David Livingstone in 1857 it was seen as the best method to civilise their colonial subjects as well as the most profitable. It was the dominant factor in relations between Britain and its African and Caribbean territories. And the justification for the expansion of those territories. It also facilitated the growth of the British missionary movement, missionaries travelling to Africa to spread this gospel.

But another age was rising in Britain. The age of Ethiopianism and Pan-Africanism. Brought to the island by Africans from the continent, the U.S. and the Caribbean. Drawn to Britain, in particular London, due to it being the centre of operations for the global colonial system. This powerful liberation movement brought to the British mainland issues of colonialism, racism, religion and equality among the races.

S.J. Celestine Edwards - Ethiopianisms' Visionary Newspaper Editor

The life and work of Samuel Jules Celestine Edwards provides us with a clear portrait of Ethiopianist activism in Britain. The existing information on his life

and work was first supplied by Peter Fryer in his book *Staying Power.* Douglas
Lorimer expanded on Fryer's work in his work *Legacies of slavery for race,
religion, and empire: S.J. Celestine Edwards and the Hard Truth* 1984. In this
publication he analyses Edwards' work as newspaper editor, author, and public
speaker, reproducing excerpts from his literature.

Born in Dominica in 1858 to liberated ex-slaves he was sent to Antigua for
his education. There he was enrolled in a Methodist school under the tutelage
of Rev Henry Mason Joseph who was to have a major influence on Edwards.
Rev Joseph went on to be a notable anti-slavery and anti-colonialism
campaigner in his own right. Travelling to the U.S. and Canada he came to
England primarily to raise money for a school in Canada populated by children
of African Americans who had escaped U.S. enslavement via the Underground
Railroad. Named the 'Wilberforce Institute' it had its' origins in the English
abolitionist movement headed by William Wilberforce. Whilst in England he
became a student in 1893, Joseph became Deputation Secretary for the Society
for the Propagation of the Gospel that same year. He went on to work with the
Society for the Recognition of the Brotherhood of Man, SRBM. Both
organisations were Christian reform groups advocating against colonialism
and racial prejudice. In 1897 he became president of the African Association,
the organising agency for the Pan-African Conference in London 1900.

Celestine Edwards' journey to England took a more complicated route. He
left Dominica aged twelve and as a sailor travelled to ports in North and South
America, and in Europe. He arrived in Edinburgh, Scotland, in the late 1870s,
then moved to Sunderland in 1880. Whilst working as a labourer he was also
a lay preacher for the Primitive Methodists, a fundamentalist Methodist group,
and a speaker for the Good Templars, a Quaker temperance society. Both these
organisations reflected Edwards concerns at that time. The Primitive
Methodists advocated a simpler more sincere Methodist practice. The
Temperance Society advocated against the sale and consumption of alcohol.
Edwards spoke out against Britain flooding its African territories, particularly
South Africa, with cheap alcohol, reaping huge profits but committing huge
damage to those communities. After failing to obtain a post as a missionary he
moved to London as a paid lecturer for the Christian Evidence Society (CES)
In London he received a diploma in Theology and undertook medical studies
at the London Hospital in Whitechapel. Whilst resident in Sunderland then
London he developed a reputation as a passionate and fluent public speaker
who at his height addressed audiences of over twelve hundred people. He
travelled to Plymouth, Bristol, Birmingham, Liverpool, Manchester,
Newcastle, and Edinburgh, mostly on behalf of the CES.

Celestine Edwards activism took off in 1892 when he founded and was editor
for *Lux,* a monthly newspaper in support of the CES. This made him the first

black editor of a national publication in Britain. In 1893 he founded another newspaper *Fraternity* of which he was also its editor. *Fraternity* was the publication of the SRBM and a successor to their previous publication Anti-Caste which was produced by Catherine Impey. Catherine Impey was an English quaker who had engaged in anti-slavery campaigns and publicised issues of racial prejudice in both the U.S. and Britain. She had links with Afro-American activists Ida B. Wells and Frederick Douglass. In 1893 Impey arranged a UK lecture tour for Ida B. Wells where she spoke of her anti-lynching campaign. Impey invited Celestine Edwards to join Ida B. Wells. Edwards paid Wells' tour expenses and arranged for the publication of her lectures in *Fraternity* newspaper under the title 'United States Atrocities'. Whilst editor of these two publications he brought to them a level of anti-racist and anti-colonialist proselytising not seen in print before. Under his leadership *Lux* and *Fraternity* published a series of articles highlighting and attacking a range of issues relating to racism, colonialism, the conditions of peoples under its rule, and the behaviour and attitudes of the colonists themselves. The newspapers also contained listings for his public speeches.

Celestine Edwards journey through these different religious organisations was not only a result of his own beliefs but a series of necessary alliances made in order to promote his message to as wide an audience as possible. The African community in Britain whilst significant was not yet large enough or organised enough to create its own anti-racist anti-colonial institutions. In the U.S. black churches such as the African Methodist Episcopal Church (AMEC) and the African Methodist Episcopal of Zion (AMEZ) grew out of large, segregated communities and provided an independent space where abolitionists and Ethiopianists could gather and transmit their messages directly to their communities. Edwards like many activists in the UK during this period had to speak through UK liberal predominantly religious organisations. In his public speeches for CES though the main subject was temperance he would use those opportunities to share experiences of his life in the West Indies and the hardship of post emancipation life for Africans in general. In November 1894 he told an audience in Newcastle:

> My ancestors proudly trod the sands of the African continent; but from their homes and friends were dragged into the slave mart and sold to the planters of the West Indies ... The very thought that my race should have been so grievously wronged is almost more than I can bear ... Of the conditions of my people today I but tarry to say that by diligence, thought, and care they have been given the lie to many a false prophet who, prior to their Emancipation, sought to convince the world that the black man was in all respects unfit for freedom ... Their position ... today is one over which I proudly rejoice. To their future I look with confidence.

Figure 17. Front and back page of *Lux* newspaper edited by S.J. Celestine Edwards 1892.

Celestine Edwards was a fervent anti-secularist. He subscribed to Ethiopianisms' vision of an African Christian nation and initially believed this could be attained through education and reform of the colonial system. His faith in the system and in the ability of the English to change their 'Anglo-Saxon' nature soon waned. He advocated Ethiopianisms' belief in Africans being agents of their own destiny, proven by their glorious past and a providential faith in a glorious future. This future he argued would be attained with or without Britain's help. He believed Christian faith and commitment were essential to the success of the abolitionist and anti-colonial movements in the face of the rampant commercialism engaged in and promoted by secularists.

An analysis of his articles in *Lux* reveals his Ethiopianist credentials and fearless radicalism. In *Lux*, August 1892 he cited statistics for the drink trade to Africa and identified it as evil as the commercially inspired slave trade. Britain was flooding Southern Africa with cheap and in some cases poisonous alcohol.

In September 1892 he published the article *Christianity and Progress* where he challenged the European secular notion that it was the enlightened rationalism of the French Revolution that was responsible for the abolition of slavery. He argued it was the efforts of enslaved Africans themselves that was the dominant factor. He cited the Haitian Revolution where enslaved Africans overthrew the former French colony as proof of this. The article was his response to the prevailing view that British intervention in African affairs was justified by the humanitarian motive of bringing enlightenment to the uncivilised masses.

In December 1892 he wrote an article entitled *This World-ism,* associating imperialism with "secularism, materialism, murder, plot, greed, incautious ambition, cupidity, lies, and caprice". And cited these as the true motivations for invading a country and "turning loose upon an indiscipline horde the weapons of civilisation".

Fraternity published letters from African American abolitionists, African Nationalists, and Caribbean writers. As well as criticisms of colonialism he also published celebrations of the successes of people of colour. Primarily heralding stories of 'Coloured Inventors, Scientists, and Good Businessmen' mainly from the U.S. but also in Britain highlighting heartening stories of everyday heroism and conviviality. *Fraternity* had its origins as *Anti-Caste,* an abolitionist journal with connections to the liberal Quaker movement in the U.S. When Edwards took over its editorship *Fraternity* magazines' primary concern was racial prejudice in the U.S. It contrasted British tolerance and humanitarianism with American racism. In Edwardian Britain this perspective was seen as a necessary tactic by African activists to get English liberals on their side, and Edwards for a while played this tactic. Despite this concession *Lux* and *Fraternity* were the most radical publications of their day and set the standard for a Pan-African press in the U.K.

During this period Edwards published his own work *From Slavery to A Bishopric* a biography of African American Bishop Walter Hawkins. Bishop Hawkins was an enslaved African who escaped his captors and fled to Canada where he received an education and eventually became Bishop of the British Methodist Episcopal Church in Canada. In his preface Edwards said of this work:

> By following Walter Hawkins from a slave farm to a Bishopric, we shall see how Providence has provided every man with the means - if he will use them - to improve his position in the world; the young Negro will see that while he may so utilise his opportunities that he shall command respect ... what Bishop Hawkins has done in one direction, millions may do in other ways.

He also used the book to detail the horrors of slavery. In the Chapter entitled *Life of A Slave* he wrote:

> The results of the institution of slavery was ... to encourage a tyrannical spirit in the masters - cast a stigma upon free labour and at once degraded and

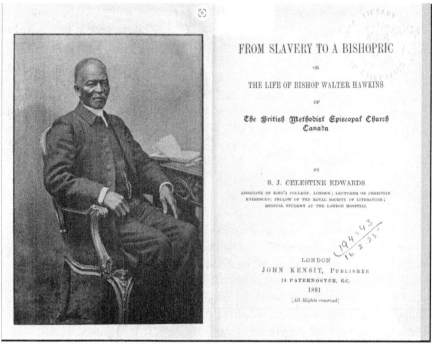

Figure 18. S.J. Celestine Edward's book *From Slavery To Bishopric.* 1891.

dehumanised the Negro. It is true that there were instances of sympathy between some masters and slaves, but unfortunately, it was more than outweighed by a long series of the most atrocious acts of cruelty, which were practised in Africa, on the voyages to America, and on the plantation.

Referring to the attitudes of enslaved Africans he wrote:

an irrepressible desire for freedom which no danger or power could restrain, no hardship deterred, and no bloodhound could alarm. This desire haunted them day and night; they talked about it to each other in confidence; they knew that the system which bound them was unjust as it was cruel, and that they ought to strive, as a duty to themselves and their children, to escape from it.

This chapter was partly in response to Liverpool slave trader James Spence's popular book *American Union* where he defended the "natural inequalities of race". Celestine Edwards also quoted from the autobiography of Frederick Douglas and from George Washington Williams' *History of the Negro Race in America* (1883) the first history of slavery by an African American. He used these works to describe the life of an enslaved African to English audiences.

Celestine Edwards attacked the idea that Blacks belonged to a different species inferior to Europeans. The Victorian era had seen the rise of 'Scientific Racism' where scientists and anthropologists made spurious 'scientific' claims to prove Black inferiority and White Superiority. He used his medical training and knowledge of Darwin's theory of natural selection to demonstrate human capacity for development. According to Edwards:

> evolutionary theory rested upon human unity and equality in origin, and the potential for progressive development under appropriate conditions. The problem was the history of slavery and of modern imperialism denied Africans and their New World descendants' opportunities to progress.

This evolutionary stance set him apart from other contributors to *Lux* as many followed the Biblical Genesis interpretation of origin.

Some of his most vociferous articles in *Lux* and *Fraternity* were attacks on current efforts of colonial expansion. In 1893 Cecil Rhodes and the British South Africa Company began the first Matebele war. In what became Rhodesia and later Zimbabwe the armed forces of Cecil Rhodes and the British South Africa Company made use of the Maxim gun to mow down the Ndebele warriors of King Logenbula. In January 1894 Edwards wrote an article *Murder will Out* mocking the celebrations in Cape Town over Rhodes conquest of the Matebele, the deathly use of machine guns, and the missionaries who supported Rhodes' war'. He wrote of it, "a war made for the express benefit of dividend-mongers". 1894 saw the British trying to expand into Uganda. The British claimed it was a humanitarian decision to stop the Islamic slave trade present in Uganda. Edwards claimed these motives as false and an attempt to fool the people of Uganda. He wrote the British presence in Uganda "would only bring more blood and additional injustice … the religion-monger is to be detested as an enemy of mankind." He cited Rhodes barbarous actions in Southern Africa as proof of Britain's real motives and ambitions. He poured scorn on the missionaries supporting these wars. In January 1894 he said of missionaries supporting Rhodes:

> if that is correct, no wonder they have so little influence over the natives for good. For not even savages can believe that war is consistent with the Christianity which Mr Rhodes missionaries proclaim.

Earlier in February 1893 he'd criticised the Church Missionary Society directly:

> we pretend to be going for the express purpose of putting down the slave trade, with a righteous indignation and horror at the wickedness of the flowers of Islam, when the truth is that we substitute a system which is worse than slavery.

These attacks on the deadly hypocrisy of missionaries and the churches that supported them was in line with Ethiopianist philosophy and practice. Secession from colonial churches as an act of African spiritual and cultural agency. His criticisms of English churches and their missionaries' involvement in the slave trade were to be validated decades later by the Church of England itself when in 2006 it apologised for its "benefiting from slave labour in the Caribbean.". As Rt Rev Tom Butler, Bishop of Southwark said:

> The profits from the slave trade were part of the bedrock of our country's industrial development. No one who was involved in running the business, financing it or benefiting from its products can say they had clean hands.

Again in 2020 the Church of England apologised, "for historic links to slavery through vicars and bishops who benefited from the barbaric practice". Within this apology it acknowledged church ownership of plantations in the West Indies and how the profits from these plantations were used to build churches and make other financial investments.

Due to his frustration with the slow pace of English anti-racists he departed from the norm of not criticising those who gave him a platform to speak. As early as 1889 he'd addressed the annual meeting of the Aborigines Protection Society. In attendance were MPs, explorers, missionaries, and humanitarians. He issued this warning:

> the misgovernment and cruel and cowardly treatment which British representatives were inflicting upon some Africans today would have to be reckoned with for with the Africans of the future. History would repeat itself. Africans did not come to this country for nothing. They frequented English slums and English palaces, and read English newspapers, and in proportion as they received education, so would their future policy take form!

The prophetic and providential nature of his warning also mirrored the Ethiopianist perspective and was a theme Edwards returned to several times in his articles; In *Lux* December 1892 he wrote:

> the injustice under which the black man is smarting will come home to his oppressors' children's children. He will surprise and disappoint those who never dreamt that the quiet happy-go-lucky black would turn like the worm upon those who wronged him. If the British nation stole no more, they have stolen enough and have sufficient responsibility at home and abroad to occupy her maternal attention for the next hundred years. If the British nation has not murdered enough no nation on God's earth has.

Two months later in the February edition he wrote:

The day is coming when Africans will speak for themselves. The day is breaking, and the despised African, whose only crime is his colour, will yet give an account of himself. We think it no crime for Africans to look with suspicion upon the European, who has stolen a part of their country, and deluged it with rum and powder, under the cover of civilisation.

The range of Celestine Edwards attacks on slavery and colonialism showed his grasp of the historical and philosophical aspects of the oppression of Africans. It also reveals him as a visionary in the causes he identified and chose to support. He challenged the twenty million pounds offered in compensation to British slaveowners at the Abolition of slavery in 1834, asking why twenty million was not given to the slaves themselves. This is the beginnings of the call for reparations made by Pan-Africanists well into the twentieth century and the formation of the Reparations movement itself.

Edwards' vision went beyond issues of race and embraced class struggle. In 1893 Edwards addressed a Trade Union march in Portsmouth. An audience of three thousand including members of the Boilermakers' Society, the General Labourers Amalgamated Union, coppersmiths, bricklayers, joiners, plasters, dockers, railway workers, stone masons, iron founders, and insurance agents. In his speech he proposed a motion for the meeting to push for the improved conditions of workers and the placement of labour representatives on all local governing bodies. He encouraged the Trade Unionists to better educate themselves through regular meetings so they could discus "the vital questions which lay at the very root of happiness and peace". He also argued that only once workers had settled their petty differences could they conduct a peaceful war against the capitalists. His appearance at Trade Union events reveals his understanding of the connection between Racial and Worker oppression, both at the hands of Capitalists.

In the October 1893 issue of *Fraternity,* he published in a set of articles called *The Angel of History.* These articles were a study of what he termed 'Anglo-Saxonism culture'. This was an attempt to examine the specific nature of English racial oppression in comparison with other national forms in the 'New World'. He compared British and American colonists with French and Spanish colonialists in the West Indies and South America. 'He found that the British and American practices were more aggressive than the French or Spanish. Whether true or not his was the first study of this nature published by an African in Britain and paved the way for later comparative studies'.

The 'Hard Truth'

By the beginning of 1894 Celestine Edwards was ill with bronchial infections. Sensing it could be terminal he threw himself into his work. He undertook a punishing lecture tour which covered Edinburgh, Aberdeen, Glasgow, Liverpool, Huddersfield, London, and Plymouth. He also wrote his masterpiece *Hard Truth* which he published in July 1894. He wrote it under pseudonym Theodore Thomas. Why he chose to use a pseudonym is unclear. The content of the book, a novella, expresses his sophisticated and unfiltered analysis of slavery and racism and of its legacy for abolitionist, humanitarian, and missionary engagements of the empire. Whether due to his increasingly bad health or ultimate frustrations with his fellow contributors to *Lux* and *Fraternity* his critique went way beyond the accepted discourse regarding Britain and race. In its preface he writes:

> There are moments though, in the lives of most men whom all the power of
> their better nature forces them to speak the Hard Truth. And after many years
> of going in and out among nations of Europe, that time of life has come to me.

Hard Truth presented a dialogue between Christ and Lucifer on slavery, emancipation, and imperialism. It emphasised the continuities from the slave past for what he termed 'Anglo-Saxonism'. It was written in three parts:

1.   Lucifer's expulsion from paradise
2.   A narrative set in Virginia of a slave girl sexually exploited by her master, and a post-emancipation murder of Caesar, an elderly literate ex-slave, and his wife by the Ku Klux Klan.
3.   A commentary on the growth of race prejudice in British culture since 1860s and of its outward extension through the new imperialism in South Africa.

The story, though set as fiction, makes several references to real life places and situations Edwards experienced in his lifetime. It begins with Christ and Lucifer arriving in South Africa. Christ is an African and Lucifer takes him on a tour of South Africa and the treatment of blacks there.

He argues the roots of racism lay in British Culture, the protestant church and their missionary outreach. contrary to its projected notion of 'fair Britain.

He drew connections between Anglo-Saxon blood and slaveholding Virginians exemplified by the Ku Klux Klan. Using the metaphor of blood as a transmitter of culture, Edwards argues that same blood drove the imperialist tendencies declaring themselves rooted in civilised Christian faith. Contrary to British ideas of 'blood purity' Edwards describes them as having Lucifer's design devil blood creating "a civilisation based on slavery, brutality, race prejudice, hatred, and destruction".

He described Lucifer as an unholy trinity of Government, Church, and people at work. This trinity:

ten million times more zealous in advancing the Kingdom of England than they are in advancing the Kingdom of God, come with great guns and shoot down the natives (who try to defend themselves with sticks), and they divide the land among themselves, and go home to the Mother Country to be decorated for bravery and good deeds.

According to Edwards Lucifer, the church had a special role. "Some good brother in your Church will come and preach 'Benevolence' to the Matabele, and their education in Sunday and day schools will be 'Servants, obey your masters!'"

In the third part entitled 'Britain leads the world' Lucifer declares 'Here's my truth; Britain is the birthplace of the very essence of the seed of prejudice against the negro race. And the little uncouth, rough shrub, when transplanted from its mother country, grows into a great tree in Gentile lands ... Furthermore, the noxious shrub owed its cultivation to British Protestantism for the churches and the missionary societies were not the agents of Christ, but the agents of Satan, as Lucifer himself affirmed throughout the book.

Hard Truth along with his articles and speeches in *Lux* and *Fraternity* represents a body of Ethiopianist philosophy never before printed and distributed in Britain. His proselytising for an African Christian nation. His belief in providence. His acknowledgement of Africa's glorious history and providential belief in a divinely delivered future. His advocation for African agency economically, politically, and spiritually. As the first Black editor of nationally distributed Newspaper, he set a high standard for black radicalism. A standard that would later be taken up by Duse Mohammad editor of The *African Times & Orient Review,* Britain's first independent black newspaper in 1912. Celestine Edwards work is firmly in the tradition of earlier Ethiopianists David Walker and Edward Blyden. His firm anti-secularism stance differentiates him from those two but his analysis of post enslavement, his scientific deconstruction of racism and colonialism places him squarely in that tradition. His was a battle between the eternal forces of good and evil in the material and spiritual world where providentially African people, the force of good, would rise again. He recognised the decline of anti-slavery sentiment in Britain since the 1860s. This he saw not just in politics but in popular culture, the rise of the minstrel show degrading the African. Added to this was his own experience of being a medical student and the prejudices faced by himself and others. He observed working class patients "with hearts as free from prejudice" requesting a Black doctor to treat them whist the "Upper Ten" class will say "Hurray up, old blackies, or niggers ... and get back to where you came from, and keep out of the way of the Maxim gun if you can".

As his health deteriorated Robert V. Allen took over editing duties on the newspaper. In May 1894 Edwards sailed for Dominica where he died 25th July

1894 at the age of thirty-four. *Fraternity* published his final article in their May 1894 edition. Under the leadership of R.V. Allen a 'Celestine Edwards Memorial Fund' was set up. Allen also became keeper of Edwards archives and continued to publish his work.

In his summation of Celestine Edwards life D. Lorimer states:

> For those supportive of Edwards through the CES, SRBM and *Fraternity,* this blight on their protestant faith prompted them to press their churches and affiliated organisations in America and overseas to comply with their vision of racial equality.

Though he worked mainly in isolation from other African activists in Britain, S.J. Celestine Edwards produced a body of work and set out an Ethiopianist philosophy that marks him out as major theorist in the evolution of Pan-Africanism in Britain. An evolution whos' theoretical lineage can be seen continued in The African Association and Pan-African Conference of 1900.

The African Association and Pan African Conference 1900

Reverend Henry Mason Joseph, Celestine Edwards' mentor during his schooling in Antigua represents a continuity of Ethiopianist thought and activism brought into the African Association, the organisation which organised the Pan African Conference of 1900. Not a lot of detail is known about him. D. Lorimer mentions him in his work on *Edwards S.J. Celestine Edwards and the Hard Truth 1894.* Mason Joseph left the Caribbean and travelled to the U.S. eventually settling in Canada where he became a teacher at the Wilberforce Institute in Chatham, Ontario, a school for children of African Americans who had escaped enslavement. He developed a reputation as a teacher and activist. It was on their behalf that he travelled to England on a fundraising trip in 1892. He stayed to study for his masters' degree whilst working for the Society for the Propagation of the Gospel, a church missionary organisation with operations in the Caribbean and Africa. He joined Edwards and Catherine Impey in London at the SRBM meeting on 11th August 1893. In 1897 he became President of the newly formed African Association.

The African Association was the brainchild of Trinidadian Henry Sylvester Williams and South African Alice Kinloch. Williams was a Trinidadian who travelled to London in 1896 to take on legal studies at Kings College. In 1897 he enrolled at Gray's Inn to study English, Latin, and English History on his way to qualifying as a barrister. Gray's Inn was a very exclusive and prestigious institution. When he joined Williams was one of only five black students there. Four were from Trinidad and one from Dominica. He would go on to meet students arriving from West Africa. His time there was very formative as he experienced first-hand the racism of the English elites whilst developing his political awareness alongside his fellow students and his activities outside the college. He struggled financially and took on paid speaking engagements with the Temperance Society and the National Thrift Society.

1897 was an important year for Williams. It was the year of Queen Victoria's diamond jubilee and London was the centre of celebrations. Royalty, Delegates and Diplomats from all corners of the empire arrived in London.

1897 was also an important year for the West Indies. The decline in the sugar trade had caused unemployment and hardship for many across the region. In March of that year a Royal Commission met in Port-of-Spain, Trinidad. Set up by Joseph Chamberlain, Secretary of State for the Colonies, heard testimony from many including Henry Alcazar, Mayor of Port-of-Spain, demanding subsidies and other economic support. The commission refused these demands thus adding to the already growing anti-colonial sentiment. Williams would have known this as he was already regularly in correspondence with Caribbean and West African publications.

Alice Kinloch. Not a lot has been written about her, but she played a crucial part in the formation of The African Association and the creation of the Pan African Conference. Born in Cape Town 1863. Her family moved to Kimberley at a time when it was experiencing huge growth due to its diamond mines. She attended mission school and excelled in her studies. Her husband Frederick Kinloch worked in the mines as an engine driver. This exposed them both to the daily working conditions of Africans mine workers.

The Kinlochs arrived in Britain in 1895. She first appears in *Fraternity* contributing to two issues in 1896. Her articles highlighted the harsh working conditions in Kimberley and other mines in South Africa. For some reason she wasn't credited by name in these articles. Celestine Edwards the editor refers to her as the 'South African lady, resident in England'. She spoke at Temperance meetings where she met H.R. Fox Bourne, Secretary of the Aboriginal Protection Society. He engaged her to speak for the Society and she did so in Manchester, Newcastle, and York. Proving herself a superb public speaker, her theme was *The ill treatment of the Natives throughout South Africa, but principally on the Compound System as obtains throughout the Mining Districts*. Her speeches were so powerful the Aboriginal Protection Society on hearing her revelations passed a resolution:

> that this meeting having heard the statements of the present position from Mrs Kinloch and Mr Fox-Bourne, calls upon Her Majesty's Government to take such action as shall effectually stop the cruel and violent measures by which the native races in South Africa and elsewhere are being deprived of their lands and liberty.

Figure 19. Plaque celebrating Alice Kinloch. Founder of the African Association and anti-colonial activist in South Africa. However, we disagree with the dates given on the plaque.

She received an invitation from Mrs Jane Cobden Unwin to speak at the Writers Club, an English organisation for progressive minded women. In her talks she explained in detail the oppressive compound system used in South Africa and Rhodesia. She wrote a nineteen-page pamphlet entitled *Are South African Diamonds Worth their cost?*. The pamphlet was published by the *Labour Press* in Manchester 1897 and distributed in South Africa. She wrote under the name A.V. Alexander, her maiden name. Her reasons for writing under a pseudonym were down to the hard-hitting nature of her writing. She described thousands of Africans going naked to work. She describes the intrusive measures used by the De Beers company to search African bodies daily. She wrote that the "old sin of Sodom" is rampant in the De Beers compound. It would have been considered indiscreet for a woman to write on such matters in such detail. Alice Kinloch's public speeches and literature brought the conditions for South Africans working in the Mining industry to the attention of British liberals.

Henry Williams and Thomas J. Thompson, whilst students at the Inns of Court contacted Mrs Kinloch and arranged a meeting with her. It was at this meeting that the idea for an Association was discussed and plans for its inception made. She agreed to become Treasurer for the Association. In correspondence with Harriet Colenso, a South African activist, Williams wrote "The Association is the result of Mrs Kinloch's work in England and the feeling that as British subjects we ought to be heard in our own affairs". Alice Kinloch herself wrote in an issue of Quaker magazine *The Friend:*

with some men of my race in this country, I have formed a society for the
benefit of our people in Africa ... I think the time has come for us to bear some
of our responsibilities, and in so doing will help the Aborigines Protection
Society.

Addressing a Quaker meeting she added "I am trying to educate people in
this country in regard to the iniquitous laws made for blacks in South Africa".
Though she and her husband returned to South Africa in 1898 she was still
active in preparations for the Pan African Conference in 1900. However, she
was unable to attend the conference person. The collaboration between Henry
S. Williams and Alice Kinloch exemplifies Ethiopianism in Britain. A
Trinidadian and South African sharing a religious based Pan-African vision.
Though initially dependent on liberal organisations as a platform to spread
their message their ultimate goal was organising their own Association and
Conference as independent entities.

The African Association was a landmark black organisation in Britain. Its'
membership was black only and it was totally independent, meaning it wasn't
dependent on white liberal or religious organisations sympathetic to its cause.
The African Association can be seen to reflect the beginnings of a transition
from Ethiopianism to political Pan-Africanism. It was the first conference
anywhere to feature the term 'Pan-African', and the term was used as a
projection of a desired future. The African Association demonstrates the
Ethiopianist philosophy of self-reliance, African agency, respect for African
culture, and an African Christian faith. This can be seen in the Associations'
founding statement:

> That in order to render the Natives under the control of Great Britain better for
> the transaction, their customs should be respected, Industrial Schools instituted
> for their benefit, and a simple and true Christianity taught them ...

Their political Pan-African vision can be seen at the beginning of the same
statement declaring its aims and objectives

> To encourage a feeling of unity to facilitate friendly intercourse among Africans
> in general; to promote and protect the interests of all subjects claiming African
> descent, wholly or in part, in British Colonies and other places, especially in
> Africa, by circulating accurate information on all subjects affecting their rights
> and privileges as subjects of the British Empire, by direct appeals to the
> Imperial and Local Governments.

Its membership at the time of formation also demonstrated its Ethiopianist
and Pan-African principles. Revd H. Mason Joseph of Antigua, President;
Thomas J. Thompson, Sierra Leone, Vice-President; Henry Sylvester

Figure 20. Henry S.
Williams. Co-founder of
the African Association
and Pan African
Conference in 1900.

Williams, Trinidad, Secretary; A.C. Durham, Trinidad, Assistant Secretary; Mrs A. Kinlock, South Africa, Treasurer. Its officers and membership were black only, though non-blacks could be awarded honorary membership. Committee members included Joseph Sydney McArthur of British Guiana, Miguel Francisco Ribeiro of Ghana, Henry Walter Reece of Barbados. Revd Charles Farquhar of Barbados who spent many years teaching in West Africa. Its 'Honorary Members and Sympathisers' included Miss F. Balgarnie. Mrs T.M. Cole, Mrs Law. And Mrs I. Fyvie Mayo. It had international support, particularly in West Africa and its formation was heralded in West African newspapers. *The Lagos Standard* implored "our countrymen to rally around the standard of the African Association". The *Lagos Weekly Record* stated, "Our people throughout Africa … give it unqualified support". The *Gold Coast Chronicle* reprinted the article published in *The Lagos Standard.* In Britain the African Association was met with messages of support from the Aborigines Protection Society, The Anti-Slavery Reporter, The Society of Friends, and the Independent Newspaper. Members of these organisations would attend AA meetings. As historian M. Sherwood wrote, "Nothing like this had ever been done before. The breadth of vision was unique"

The Pan African Conference 1900

The African Association changed its name at the beginning of 1900 to the Pan African Association in preparation for its conference. It had branches in Jamaica, Trinidad and the U.S. The 3-day conference took place at Westminster Town Hall, London between 22nd - 24th July 1900. The Ethiopianist input can be seen in its attendees and participants who arrived from the U.S. The Caribbean, Africa, and Britain itself. It was chaired by Bishop Alexander Walters head of the AMEC. It also had women delegates, a very progressive move at that time. Two African American women spoke at the conference. Anna J. Cooper, formerly enslaved, was a member of the American Negro Academy, and a leading educator and human right activist. She was author of a very influential book *Voice from the South by a Black Woman from the South.* Anna H. Jones, a Canadian born suffragist, was also a key speaker. She delivered a presentation *A Plea for Race Individuality.* Two other female attendees were African American sisters Ella D. Barrier and Fanny Barrier Williams, both educators, members of the Coloured Womens' League, and activists for Womens' rights.

The Pan-African Conference had 5 stated aims:

1.   To secure for Africans throughout the world true civil and political rights.

2.   To ameliorate the condition of our brothers on the continent of Africa, America, and other parts of the world.

3.   To promote efforts to secure effective legislation and encourage our people in educational, industrial, and commercial enterprise.

4.   To foster the production of writing and statistics relating to our people everywhere.

5.   To raise funds for forwarding these purposes.

Papers delivered at the conference included: *The Trials and Tribulations of the Coloured Race in America* (Bishop Alexander Walters) *Conditions Favouring a High Standard of African Humanity* (C.W. French of St. Kitts) *The Preservation of Racial Equality* (Anna Cooper of the U.S.) *The Necessary Concord to be Established between Native Races and European Colonists* (Benito Sylvain. Haitian aide-de-camp to the Ethiopian emperor) *Africa, the Sphinx of History* (D.E. Tobias of the U.S.) *The Progress of Our People in Light of Current History* (John E. Quinlan of St. Lucia) Other topics written

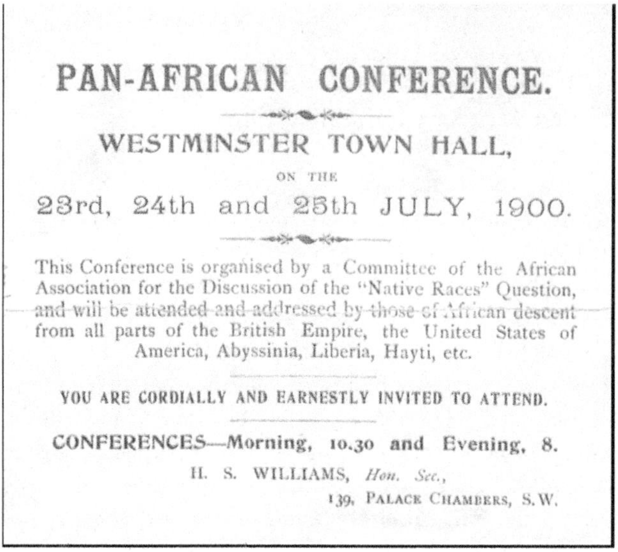

PAN-AFRICAN CONFERENCE.

WESTMINSTER TOWN HALL,

ON THE

23rd, 24th and 25th JULY, 1900.

This Conference is organised by a Committee of the African
Association for the Discussion of the "Native Races" Question,
and will be attended and addressed by those of African descent
from all parts of the British Empire, the United States of
America, Abyssinia, Liberia, Hayti, etc.

YOU ARE CORDIALLY AND EARNESTLY INVITED TO ATTEND.

CONFERENCES—Morning, 10.30 and Evening, 8.

H. S. WILLIAMS, *Hon. Sec.,*
139, PALACE CHAMBERS, S.W.

Figure 21. Advert for
the Pan-African
Conference in London
1900.

and discussed included: Pseudo-scientific racism. The war in Southern Africa.
Reparations for Africa and Africans.

The Pan-African Conference symbolically marks the adoption of the term
Pan-African by anti-colonial and black liberation groups. Though the term
'Ethiopianism' would still be in use for a few more years 'Pan-African' became
the umbrella term. We see within the aims and declarations of the Pan African
Conference the principles of Ethiopianism which preceded it.

After the conference Henry S. Williams launched the first issue of his journal
The Pan-African appearing in London October 1901. It stated its ambition to
be "the mouthpiece of the millions of Africans and their descendants… to
chronicle facts relative to the race's progress and welfare". There were two
further issues published by these have since disappeared. We know this
through reviews of them in the Trinidadian press. He is known to have also
written *The British Negro,* a reprinting of two lectures on the subject but again
there is no known existing copy. Despite the short life of *The Pan-African*
Williams continued his activism in Britain and abroad. In London he ran for
office believing there should be an African spokesman in Parliament. He joined
the Fabian Society and the National Liberal Club but failed to get elected as an
MP. He did however get elected on to the Marylebone Borough Council in
1906. He would return to Trinidad where he died in 1911.

CHAPTER THREE: PASSING THROUGH, SOWING SEEDS - ETHIOPIANIST STUDENT ACTIVISM IN BRITAIN

"Nowhere can one get such a good idea of what is happening in all parts of the world as in London... the English colonial system brings every year hundreds of representations of all races and colours from every part of the world to London" So said the great African American leader Booker T. Washington writing from London in 1899.

The end of the nineteenth and beginning of the twentieth centuries saw a rise in the Black population of Britain and the number of black students arriving in the U.K. They came from all corners of the Empire in search of educational opportunities denied to them in their homelands. They brought with them a determination to be agents of change. They brought with them Ethiopianism.

Who and Where Were They?

West Africa provided the highest number of students in Britain during this period. It's history as a British colonial territory was older and its' colonial structures were more developed than other parts of Africa. By the turn of the twentieth century West Africa had a substantial black middle class. Its adoption and promotion of Ethiopianism was primarily through the U.S. based African Methodist Episcopal Church of Zion, and the philosophies of Edward Blyden, Bishop James Horton, J.C. Casely-Hayford, and many more. These philosophies were often presented under the guise of West African Nationalism. They flourished in what would become Ghana, Nigeria, Sierra Leone, Gambia where ideas such as a unified West African Church, and West African University were attempted. Ethiopianism in West Africa had its own character. It didn't practice the secessions from European churches on the scale seen in Southern Africa. Interestingly West Africans mainly used the term in reference to themselves and not African Americans. Casely-Hayford wrote "It is not so much Afro-Americans we want as Africans or Ethiopians". Hayford, a stout Ethiopianist, in this statement was also expressing the nationalist tendencies of West Africa. Students arriving in Britain came out of this environment. They were usually from the educated African elite.

Southern Africa was a more fertile ground for Ethiopianism of a more ecclesiastical nature. This saw the rise of African Independent Churches and

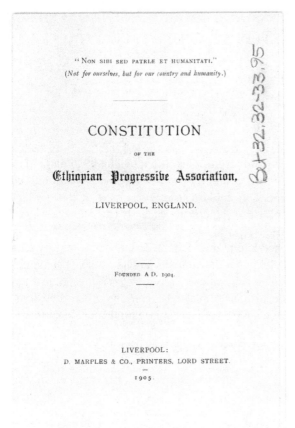

Figure 22. Front page of the Ethiopian Progressive Association constitution.

the movement to secede from European churches. Missionary schools such as Healdtown and Lovedale were fertile grounds for black radical thought and many students from these schools entered the political activist arena in Southern Africa and Britain. The colonial wars between the Boers, British, Zulus, Xhosa, and Shona. The creation of 'Rhodesia' by Cecil Rhodes and the European drive to create a similar state apartheid in South Africa occupied the minds and hearts of Southern African students based in Britain.

Students arrived from the Caribbean at a time when the region was grappling with a failing economy and mass unemployment due to the near collapse of the sugar industry. Ethiopianism as an ecclesiastical force took the form of independent Zionist and Ethiopianist churches led by radical preachers who led a largely nomadic existence. It didn't have the organisational structured presence seen in Africa and the U.S. Despite this, the anti-colonial movement flourished producing some of the key figures in the black nationalist movement, many of them students.

What was the Role of these students in Britain?

The students had experienced a colonial education in their homelands that presented Britain as a benevolent civilising force and initially some conformed to that perception. Their experiences in Britain, the belly of the colonial beast, brought many of them face to face with a harsh reality in contradiction to this myth. The circumstances of their time in Britain forced them to challenge the racist ideas and behaviours they faced there. Any illusion of British moral superiority was quickly removed. They had their own Ethiopianist motives for coming as articulated by South African student Pixley Seme in 1906,

> those who studied abroad learnt that 'knowledge is power'… you find them in Edinburgh, in Cambridge, and in the good schools of Germany. These return to their countries like arrows, to drive darkness from the land.

The darkness was the colonial system, and they as the arrows were guided by the Ethiopianist missionary imperative. That is, to travel to the highest learning institutions and gather what was necessary to liberate and develop their parts of Africa. They did this through organising on behalf of their homelands and articulating their demands directly to the British public and ruling class. They acted as intermediaries between African communities and their colonial masters in London. They enlisted British church and reformist groups into their campaigns, using these groups as a vehicle to preach their liberation ideologies. They used their homeland connections to argue on their behalf their own case for equal rights in Britain. The role of West and Southern African native organisations in petitioning the British educational and government institutions is well documented. They campaigned for better treatment of their 'colonial subjects' in Britain. They created vital networks with other black students and activists. This was a vital and impactful role played by students. They formed Pan-African networks with their African, West Indian, and U.S. counterparts. Through these networks they expanded their knowledge of the black global experience and found common focus hosting conferences, events, and building organisations together. Their time in Britain also brought them into direct contact with Britain's growing trade union movement. Reformist ideas such as Socialism were taking in root in Britain and would grow to influence a host of resident black student activists. Their embrace of these ideas formed the basis for what would later be termed 'African Socialism'.

Where Did They Study?

Edinburgh, Liverpool, and Oxford Universities were all hubs for black student activism. At Edinburgh University in Scotland, they formed the Afro-West

Figure 23. The Afro-West Indian Literary Society in Edinburgh University.

Indian Literary Society and the West African Medical Students Association. Liverpool University students formed the Ethiopian Association and the Ethiopian Progressive Association. At Oxford University they formed an African Students Club which changed its name to the African Union Society. In London black students at the prestigious law schools Gray's Inn and Lincoln's Inn were very active in anti-colonial organisations and activities. Many fulfilled their aim of gaining legal qualifications then returning to their native lands to practice on behalf of their people. In Colwyn Bay in Wales a unique institution for black education was formed. The African Institute, also known as 'Congo House', was founded by a radical Welsh Missionary Revd William Hughes. Young boys from the Congo and South Africa came to receive an Ethiopianist education in Law, Medicine, and Industrial skills. It became a meeting point for black activists and many of its students went on to do great things in England and their homelands.

What Strategies did they use?

West African Students were heavily involved in activism at Edinburgh University. In 1898 They and other black students had formed The Afro-West Indian Literary Society of Edinburgh University. The Society's stated object was "the promotion of social life and intellectual improvement among African and West Indian students in Edinburgh" To this effect they lobbied politicians and wrote to the press in both Britain and West Africa. Membership was open to "to all African and West Indian students and others that the Committee approves of. They sent a number of delegates to the Pan-African Conference. William Meyer, a Trinidadian medical student. John Alcindor, a Trinidadian graduate of Edinburgh Medical school in 1899. Richard Akiwande Savage, medical student and vice-president of the Society. Meyer presented a paper to the Conference attacking 'pseudo-scientific racism. "For trying to prove the Negroes were worthless and depraved persons who had no right to live". Alcindor remained in London and would go on to make a name for himself as both a doctor and an activist being one of the founder members of the African Progress Union becoming its' president in 1921. Richard Akiwande Savage was a member of the University student Representative Council 1898-1900. He eventually returned to West Africa where he became editor of *The Gold Coast Leader,* a leading newspaper in support of Ethiopianism and Pan-Africanism in West Africa and Britain. The Afro-West Indian Literary Society provided an important social function for black students as they faced racism in the form of a colour-bar within the University and from the city of Edinburgh itself.

In 1900 West African medical students erupted in outrage at a decree made by Colonial Secretary Joseph Chamberlain. Chamberlain had decreed that Africans were no longer to be employed as West African Medical staff, because they were "not judged as competent as Europeans". The policy would allow them to practice only on 'natives', usually in sub-standard conditions, and thus be a barrier to them attaining their highest professional practice. They petitioned the Dean of the Faculty of Medicine, and the University Principal Sir William Turner to complain on their behalf. Letters were sent out to Chamberlain, local MP Sir John Batty Tuke. Chamberlain ignored these petitions. Britain was in the process of expanding and consolidating its territories in the region, a unification which ultimately led to the creation of the state of Nigeria in 1914. This process of consolidation was enacted by means of open warfare. The maxim gun being the decisive weapon used against the indigenous peoples. The students' actions show their political links with West Africa and their ability to organise at the highest level.

Other West African medical students involved in activism whilst at Edinburgh University include Moses Da Roche, a Nigerian who went on to become Assistant Secretary of the African Association with Henry Williams.

In 1906 Herbert Christian Bankole-Bright was a Nigerian medical student at Edinburgh. He was from an elite West African family and had received a strict religious education. As a student he was politically active writing letters attacking colonialism. He participated in debates hosted by the Afro-West Indian Association and was an acclaimed public speaker. He'd written to Keir Hardie, co-founder of the British Labour Party in support of Hardie's criticisms

Figure 24. H.C.
Bankole-Bright.
Nigerian Medical
student at Edinburgh
University. Practised
medicine in London
whilst advocating
against colonial rule.

of British misrule in Africa and Hardy had responded. Publication of Hardie's letter to Bankole-Bright, known as the 'Zulu Letter' caused questions about colonial rule and mistreatment of the natives to be raised in Parliament. Bankole-Bright qualified and for five years practised medicine at the Royal Infirmary in Edinburgh and the London Hospital. In 1910 he returned to Africa setting up a medical practice in Freetown, Sierra Leone, and went on to become one of the founders of the National Congress of British West Africa, and the Ethiopianist group 'West African Students Union' in Britain.

Another West African medical student to leave his mark in Britain was Bandele Omoniyi, a radical reformer firmly in the Ethiopianist tradition. Born in Lagos, Nigeria in 1884 Omoniyi differed from other Ethiopianists of that period as he was one of the first to embrace Socialism and his writings foretold the rise of 'African Socialism' among African students in the following decades. He travelled to Liverpool in 1905 to study medicine. There he connected with members of the Ethiopian Progressive Association and made a name for himself as his political writing took off. He wrote to *The Lagos Standard* demanding support for the Ethiopian Progressive Association, an organisation that looked to teach "our governments that taxation without representation is tyrannical" He enrolled in Edinburgh University in 1906 but stayed only a year giving up his studies to "devote himself to literary work in support of the claims of his countrymen" Whilst in Edinburgh he became secretary of Joseph Booth's British Christian Union for West and Central Africa. Joseph Booth was a radical English missionary based in Malawi whos' belief in radical egalitarianism brought him into conflict with colonialists and fellow missionaries.

In 1906 in the state of Natal in South Africa an armed uprising known as the Bambata Rebellion broke out against government forces. Ethiopianism had a strong base in Natal and the rebellion led to the British and colonial press to fiercely attack the movement positioning it as 'agent provocateur' among the natives. Omoniyi's response was to write his ground-breaking book *In Defence of the Ethiopianism Movement*. The book was a defence of the movement arguing the roots of the Bambata and other rebellions lay in the unjust policies of the colonial forces. It also gives insight into Omoniyi's own brand of Ethiopianism. He argues for reform of the British Empire allowing more access and opportunities for educated black elites and warns of the consequences of not doing so.

> The present system of government has some fatal defects which at some near or distant time must bring disaster not only to the government but to the people on whose behalf it rules... the British children at no distant generation will and must pay the full penalty which their fathers have purchased for them by regulating their duty and obligations to the people of Africa ...

He goes on to state his own allegiance to British principles of rule.

> ... I have never attempted, nor will I ever attempt to prove that the British rule is either unjust or impartial. But I have said and will say that the British representatives have been unfaithful to the charge committed to them ...

He attacks the implementation of British rule not its basic right to. But this allegiance had its limits

> If the black man be taught to look upon the white man as a friend and a neighbour, and not as a marauder and plunderer, and if respect for the British rule be cultivated in him rather than dread of it, there need not be any fear... but if the present state of things were to continue in which he simply lives in dread of the white man's maxim guns, the least chance that he may have will be used in plotting against those he lives in constant dread of, and who can say what tomorrow may bring ...

For Omoniyi, self-rule did "not in any way imply secession from the Mother Country". Hakim Adi summarises Bandele Omoniyi's body of work:

> Omoniyi produced a body of work that envisaged a British empire where black Edinburgh doctors continued to play a prominent role, at the same time as he demanded freedom of speech, absolute equality before the law, and an end to job discrimination, economic exploitation and military intervention; the abolition of hut and poll taxes, the widening of the franchise in the colonies, and an increase in the number of African members of the legislative councils, and defended the black nationalist Ethiopianist Movement so that a "renovated Africa will take her place amongst the nations of the world.

Omoniyi's time in Britain exposed him to socialism. He wrote articles and corresponded with the Labour Leader of the Independent Labour Party. He wrote to members of the government, and Keir Hardie and Ramsey Macdonald co-founders of the Labour Party. He explored the subject in his book *Socialism Examined* 1906 he linked socialism to "Equality of freedom and opportunity of all races!" In an article entitled *The Labour Question in Africa* in *The Lagos Times* he compelled readers to:

> compare the conditions and treatments of the working classes in all the departments all over the coasts of Africa with those in other places and thereby try with all possible efforts to insure a change of condition of things for better.

He claimed that the duty to improve the lives of the African working class "rests principally upon themselves and is mainly dependent on their realising that 'Unity is Strength …one great community for the general good of Africa'. The Ethiopianism of Bandele Omoniyi 'One great community for the general good of Africa' mirrored aspects of Marcus Garvey's 'One God, One Aim, One Destiny'. Omoniyi died under mysterious circumstances in Brazil in 1912. His importance lies in his defence of Ethiopianism which he described as:

> a struggle between those who recognise their claims to an equal participation in social and political rights with others, and those who for themselves and their order assert a certain fictitious superiority of race, and claim for it as a consequence of causes, however accidental, exclusive consideration and special privileges and immunities, who are being impelled to this injustice and impolicy by the aggrandisement of power, the tendency of the greater to swallow up the less.

The South African Zulu Choir

The scope of Ethiopianist activism among South Africans went beyond the overtly political and embraced cultural activism. This can be seen in the activities of South African Zulu Choir that visited and performed in Britain during the last decade of the nineteenth and first decade of the twentieth centuries. An examination of their motives and their experiences in Britain give us an insight into the dilemmas faced by politicised Africans in Britain and how they dealt with them.

A choir from South Africa named the 'African Choir' arrived in Britain in 1891. They were made up of fifteen students from Kimberley Missionary school and Lovedale Missionary Institute located in the Cape Province region. Both these institutions were relatively progressive schools for African students. Lovedale, founded in the early 1820s, went on to produce highly politicised graduates who went on to become prominent political figures in South Africa history. Steve Biko, Chris Hani, and Ellen Kuzwayo were all ex-students of Lovedale. As students of Kimberley and Lovedale the choir represented the educated elite of black Africans. They wanted to present themselves accordingly to their British white middle class audiences. However, on arrival

Figures 26 *(top)* and 27 *(bottom)*. The South African Zulu Choir arrived in London 1891. They performed in both Victorian and African attire.

they discovered the expectations of the audiences and their tour promoters clashed with these own ideas. These expectations can be best described as:

> By the late nineteenth century, the British had a long history of outing black people on stage and had evolved stock roles for them to play. Blacks could be freaks, savages, angels, minstrels, slaves and warriors and were variously used to instil fear, loathing, compassion, wonder or sexual delight.

Photographs of the choir in 1891 show them in full Victorian dress, as would have been worn by the educated classes. Upon arrival they embarked on a tiring touring schedule the length of England into Scotland and Ireland. They were invited to perform for Queen Victoria on the Isle of Wight. Their repertoire consisted of traditional songs, Christian hymns, and English ballads. After a few performances they decided to wear traditional dress for the first half of their performance and Victorian dress for the second half. Whilst they no doubt had pride in their traditional dress this led to their performance being dubbed 'Africa Civilised and Africa Uncivilised'. Such was the attitude of a colonial minded press. "Judging by the correspondence between London and Cape Town around this issue of sartorial representation, would not have been made without a lot of soul-searching". The motives of the members to come to Britain and tour gives us clues. The *Christian Express* a monthly periodical published in South Africa wrote:

> The Choir was organised with the professed object of deepening and extending the widespread interest in Africa and the African and of endeavouring to show the capability of the South African in a novel direction.

Choir member, Charlotte Mange, when interviewed in London, September 1891, claimed the tour was a fund-raising expedition.

> Let us be in Africa even as you are in England ... Help us to found schools for which we pray, where our people could learn to labour, to build; to acquire your skill with our hands.

Her vision was to raise funds for a technical school in Kimberley where the recent development of diamond mining had increased the mainly illiterate black workforce. In the same interview she insisted her main motivation was to persuade the English to take action against the encroaching power of the emerging settler class in South Africa and the ruthlessness of the Boers. Other motives within the group were less political. One member Paul Xinwine, a wealthy businessman and entrepreneur from Cape Town, saw profit as his main motive. He challenged the political motives of other members "The venture of the choir was a monetary speculation in spite of all the platform declarations".

Figure 28. London newspaper article on members of the 'African Native Choir'. This is the same ensemble also known as the South African Zulu Choir.

A 'Platform declaration' was the appeal made to the audience at the end of each performance for funds. Xinwine was to suffer badly in his profit-making efforts in the face of English racism. He'd personally invested in the tour and was furious when refused representation on the management committee of the choir. He would later write of the two promoters/managers Balmer and Letty:

> I advanced them £30 or its' equivalent of which they only paid me five. In the same way another member of the choir lent them £100 at Kimberley and goodness knows if he will ever recover it. They [the English managers] say they can show their books and accounts in order to prove that they have been losing money. It is a perfectly easy thing to put any figures in books! Why, you have false balance sheets with banks which are supposed to have strict and proper auditors. How much easier for a body of men who are their own auditors.

These differences in motives caused recrimination within the group exacerbated by lack of pay from their English management who blamed the souring costs of the tour for their inability to pay what had been promised. Paul Xinwine and his wife Eleanor left the tour in early 1892 returning to South Africa. Other members soon followed. Those who remained continued to tour until management finally abandoned them penniless in a cheap London hotel. They were eventually rescued by the Missionary Society who raised funds to send them home. In 1893 Charlotte Mange and a small number of the original choir would regroup and embark on a tour of the U.S. once again managed by Balmer and Letty.

Here we see some of the obstacles faced by those who came to Britain with an Ethiopianist motive. The need to satisfy to varying degrees the patronising demands of liberal Victorianism who they were dependent on. The internal differences of motives within the group. The risk of being swindled by English entrepreneurs driven by the same exploitative attitudes towards Africans as their colonial counterparts in South Africa. The African Choir were the educated elite of the Cape Town province. They arrived in Britain filled with an Ethiopianist vision of presenting themselves through their artform as the vanguard of African self-reliance and self-development. They used the English Victorian fascination with Africa, however misguided, to call for action in their homeland. They returned to Africa battered and bruised by their experiences but not beaten, as Charlotte Mange's regrouping and subsequent tour of the U.S. shows.

Figure 29. Charlotte Mange depicted on a 1890 Christmas card. Co-Founder of the African Zulu Choir and the Bantu Women's League in South Africa.

Charlotte Mange (also called Maxeko)

Charlotte Mange, went on to find the Bantu Women's League and become a prominent activist for women's rights in South Africa. She also campaigned for representation of women in the newly formed African National Congress.

The South African musical connection with Britain again reveals Ethiopianist motives when we look at members of the 'African Zulu Choir' who toured Britain 1892-93. Saul Msane, Josiah Gumede, and Solomon Khumalo were all members of the choir. They were supported during their stay by the Brotherhood, an amalgamation of British reformist institutions such as the Aboriginal Protection Society, the Anti-Slavery Society, and the Quakers. Saul Msane returned to South Africa and formed the Natal Natives Congress. He visited Britain again in 1914 as a delegate in the South Africa Native National Congress (SANNC). Gumede was to become future president of the ANC. Khumalo joined John Booth's African Christian Union and became an advocate its Pan-African vision.

Ethiopianism in Music and Entertainment in Britain

London as cultural capital of the empire attracted black musicians and artists from all its territories. However, one London born musician/composer rose above all others in fame and accomplishments. Samuel Coleridge-Taylor was the pre-eminent classical composer and musician of his day. Born in Holborn, London in 1875. His father was from Sierra Leone who'd come to London, qualified as a medical surgeon before travelling to Gambia to be its Chief Coroner. Not much is known of his English Mother. By his mid-twenties he'd written a stream of compositions culminating in his most famous *Hiawatha's Wedding Feast* written in 1898. This choral-orchestral work was far and away the most popular classical composition in Britain right up to 1912. The titles of his other works reveal his political ideals. *African Suite* in 1898, *African Romances* in 1897 (A collaboration with the African American poet Paul Laurence Dunbar), *Ethiopia saluting the Colours* in 1902, *Four African Dances* in 1902, *Twenty-Four Negro Melodies* in 1904, *Symphonic Variations on an African Air* in 1906. As his titles suggest Coleridge-Taylor strived to incorporate African settings and melodies into classical musical and was very successful at it.

It is his lesser celebrated work as an activist that marks him out as a major black British presence in Edwardian Britain. He met Paul Laurence Dunbar in London in 1896 and the two performed music and poetry collaborations together. In 1898 he was introduced to Frederick J. Loudin, former director of

Figure 30. Flyer for the *In Dahomey* musical in London in 1903.

the celebrated Fisk Jubilee Singers. They were a pioneering African American choir rooted in the U.S. Ethiopianist tradition that had toured Britain in 1875. Coleridge-Taylor's own experiences of racism in the highly elitist world of British classical music had already impacted on him. He worked alongside H. Sylvester Williams as an elected member of the Pan-African Association. He was in charge of the musical side of the programme at the Pan-African Conference in 1900. Speaking of his life in London he said "As for the prejudice, I am well prepared for it … I am a great believer in my race, and I never lose an opportunity of letting my white friends know it …" Fame brought him to the U.S. many times during the 1900s. There he met W.E. Dubois and Booker T. Washington and soaked up their Pan-African ideas. Back in London he would later contribute articles to the *African Times and Orient Review,* the first independent black owned newspaper in Britain. In its' first issue in July 1912, he said of it,

> There is of course, a large section of the British people interested in the coloured races, but it is, generally speaking, a commercial interest only … Therefore, it is imperative that this venture be heartily supported by the coloured people themselves, so that it shall be absolutely independent of the whites as regards circulation.

No doubt Samuel Coleridge-Taylor would have been in the audience for "the most popular musical show in London" in 1903. The staging of an African American musical *In Dahomey.* The first full length all black musical it had launched earlier that year to large audiences in the U.S. Its' commercial success was despite the hostility of the white press. *The New York Times* report citing it as "an initiation of a potential race war". The music was by celebrated musical theatre composer Will Marion Cook with lyrics by Paul Laurence Dunbar it starred Bert Williams and George Walker, two of the biggest black vaudeville performers in the U.S. who choreographed and performed the celebrated and much copied dance routines. It played at the prestigious Shaftesbury Theatre in London. After which it toured England culminating with a performance at Buckingham Palace in front of the Royal family. *In Dahomey: A Negro Musical Comedy* was a satire on the American Colonization Society's 'back to Africa movement' on the U.S. earlier that century. It tells the story of two African Americans who suddenly and accidently become wealthy and decide to emigrate back to Africa with a group of African American emigrants. It was the first time these themes and ideas had appeared in musical theatre which at the time was the most popular form of entertainment for the masses. It returned to U.S. for further tours. Its' performers Williams and Walker would create two further musicals named *In Abyssinia* and *In Bandana Land.*

Coleridge-Taylor's deliberate use of African melodies allied to the titles he gave to his compositions. *In Dahomey's* comedic exploration of repatriation and the 'back to Africa' movement. Both are in tune with the Ethiopianist discourse taking place both in the U.S. and in Britain. Coleridge-Taylor was fluent in the Nationalist ideas of West Africa and the U.S. Paul Laurence Dunbar was a founder member of the 'Harlem Renaissance', a radical group of black artists and writers in the U.S. That they both flourished in London is in part due to the black networks there they were part of. These two musical examples, alongside the Choirs that visited, show the methods used to transmit Ethiopianism were not limited to political protest but involved cultural activism via artistic expression at the turn of the century.

From Congo to Colwyn Bay via Cape Town - The African Institute

In September 1909 a Brotherhood Orchestra based in north London performed at the Brotherhood national conference in Cardiff. Theirs was a farewell performance for the black South African delegates who'd attended the conference and were due to sail home. One of the musicians in the Orchestra was Davidson Don Tengo Jabavu, a South African activist whose story reveals another strand of Ethiopianism on Britain.

D. D. T. Jabavu's story begins in 1885 in South Africa where he was born to John Tengo Jabavu and Elda Sakuba. His father had gained fame as a political activist and newspaper editor. In 1881 he became editor of their xhosa-language journal *Isigidimi samaxhosa* (The Xhosa Messenger) In 1884 he became editor of his own newspaper, South Africa's first independent newspaper written in Xhosa language *Imvo Zabantsunda* (Black Opinion).

In 1885 Davidson Don Tengo Jabavu was born. His father sent him to Lovedale Mission school. After completing his school education his father tried to enrol him in Dale College, a white college. Despite passing the entrance exams Davidson was refused admission. The college authorities, whilst expressing regret, had declined to admit him on the grounds that if they did so many European parents would remove their sons from the college "My boy is now at college in England" "I had no wish to send him there, but I had no other choice". This raises the question of why did John Tengo Jabavu, by now a major political and educational figure in Cape Town, send his son overseas to Colwyn Bay in Wales?

The African Institute in Colwyn Bay, Wales, also known as 'Congo House' or the 'Congo Training Institute' was a unique example of an Ethiopianist educational institute in Britain. It was the brainchild of Reverend William Hughes. Hughes was a radical Baptist minister and proud Welsh nationalist. He resented the colonisation of Welsh culture and language by the English as well their taking over the administration of Wales itself. In 1882 he travelled to Bayneston in Congo to join the Baptist missionary there. He clashed with missionary authorities over their attitudes to the natives. Forced to leave the mission he returned to Wales in 1885 determined to set up his own missionary school according to his principles. In 1900 the 'African Institute' opened its doors to African students. The idea was African students would attend, study law, medicine, and industrial skills in order to return to support their communities. In the twelve years it opened students came from Cameroon, Nigeria, Sierra Leone, South Africa, and the U.S. Over 100 students would attend.

The Institute also attracted Ethiopianist and Pan-African visitors who would meet and discuss current affairs. Davidson Don Tengo Jabavu studied at the Africa Institute. In 1906 he left to attend the Universities of London and Birmingham where he earnt a B.A in English. After completing his studies, he travelled to the U.S. where he met with Booker T. Washington at his Tuskegee Institute. Upon returning to South Africa, he set up the South African Native College at Fort Hare in Cape Province. It was the first higher education institute in South Africa built for black people. One of Jabavu's students was a young man named Nelson Mandela, future President of South Africa.

Figure 32. 'Congo House' in Colwyn Bay, Wales.

Figure 33. Rev William Hughes, his wife, staff, and students at the Africa Institute.

Davidson Don Tengo Jabavu's journey to Colwyn Bay and subsequent activism in his homeland was mirrored by its other students. Students returned to Africa and practised law, medicine, teaching, and founded newspapers. One ex-student, Oladipo Lahamini, stayed in Britain and went on to be one of the founders of the West African Students Association in London. When one sees the type of student that passed through The African Institute, John Tengo Jabavu's decision to send his son Davidson there makes sense. Davidson went on to achieve professional qualifications denied to him in South Africa. He widened his Pan-African network and returned to apply those values in his homeland.

An interesting footnote. Five students died whilst at Congo House. They were buried in the local cemetary in Colwyn Bay. Every year a delegation of dignatories and relatives of the deceased from the Congo joins a Welsh delegation in a procession from the school to the cemetary. They tend the graves They hold a service in honour of the young student. The last procession was held in 2016.

Other Prominent Ethiopianist Student Activists

Other South Africans, students and professional, left their Ethiopianist mark on Britain. Dr Henry Barton Gabashane. He was a representative member of the Ethiopian Progressive Association based in Liverpool formed in 1904. In 1898 Gabashane had, like many South Africans driven by an Ethiopianist imperative, travelled to the U.S. His trip was sponsored by the African Methodist Episcopal Church, the largest Ethiopianist church in America. After five years he arrived in Liverpool and enrolled in the University as a medical student. He became active with the Ethiopian Progressive Association. The Ethiopian Progressive Association was formed by West African and West Indian students at the various colleges in the city. They published a journal *The Ethiopian Review* in 1905 but no copies remain. The organisation folded in 1905 after which Gabashane returned to South Africa and set up a medical practice in Swaziland.

Isaac Pixley Seme from Natal entered Jesus College, Oxford University to study Law in 1907 with the declared intention of becoming 'Attorney-General for his people'. His journey from Natal to Oxford, was via New York where he studied at Columbia University. Whilst at Oxford he organised an African Students Club which soon changed its name to the African Union Society, a body "which was open to all men of African or Negro extraction who are interested in the general welfare of the Race both in Africa and other parts of the world". Sadly, the African Union Society didn't last very long, but while he was at Oxford he established a network of like-minded activists including

Figure 34. Isaac Pxley Seme. South Africa student at Oxford University where he formed the African Union Society 1907.

Alain Locke from the U.S. and Dr Theophilus Scholes from Trinidad, Dr William Awooner-Renner from Sierra Leone, and Albert Mangena who became Seme's legal partner. By this time Seme's reputation was high mainly due a speech he'd made in New York entitled *The Regeneration of Africa.* The speech was widely circulated in the U.S. press. It was reprinted in the *Journal of the African Society* and in South Africa. He graduated from Oxford and was called to the bar in 1910. He'd moved to London in 1908 where he immersed himself in its Pan-Africanist networks. In 1909 Seme and Albert Mangena were asked by the Transvaal Native Congress to act on their behalf and challenge the racist South African Bill about to come before parliament. He met with the South African delegation who'd travelled to London to oppose the bill. By 1910 Seme and Mangena had returned to Johannesburg where they set up a legal practice.

Albert Mangena was a law student in Britain. Born in 1879 and raised in Cape Province he attended Mission school and began a teaching career. By 1899 he was articulating African claims for a 'Universal Franchise'. Following the invasion of the Cape colony by the British in 1900 he was advocating for Natives rights and dedicated to the study of law. He travelled to London in 1902 and by 1904 he was elected a member of the recently founded African Society. Membership gave him access to the African network in London where he met fellow activists Joseph Gumede. Through his legal studies at Lincoln Inn, he met Moses Taylor and Akilagpa Gosford Sawyer both from Sierra Leone. Peter Sampson, Joseph Eminsang and John Theo Holm from the Gold Coast. Thomas Brem Wilson, Albert S. Cann, and A. Kwesi Bhoma. Mangena, who closely followed events in his Natal homeland called these activists together at a meeting in High Holborn, London, to protest at these events. The purpose of the meeting was

> to discuss ways and means by which a society could be formed ... to promote friendly intercourse amongst 'coloured' races coming to Europe, to render mutual help, discuss social and political subjects connected with the race, and to work in such ways as the society when formed may think would be conducive to the progress of Africans, and to the advancement of the Africans.

From this meeting was formed the United African Association.

Back home in Natal the government had imposed Martial Law in response to native protests and imposed the death sentence on twelve protesters after the death of two white policemen. Mangena, through the United African Association's protested these actions to the Colonial Office and the Privy Council. They instigated legal proceedings against the Governor of Natal Sir Henry McCallum. News of Mangena's activities in London reached Natal. The governor Sir McCallum used the Criminal Investigation Department to gather

PART 1.

... THE ...

EARTH A PLANE.

BY

JOHN EDWARD QUINLAN

(Commissioned Land Surveyor of St. Lucia and St. Vincent,
British West Indies).

7, CHARLWOOD PLACE, PIMLICO, LONDON, S.W.

Figure 35. John E. Quinlan, St. Lucian contributor the P.A.C. Author and advocate for the rights of Caribbean people.

evidence against him and disseminated falsities in an effort to discredit him. Articles appeared in the *The Times* and the *Daily Chronicle* impugning his character. Mangena launched a series of libel cases against them. Though he ran out of finances and had to rely on the support of friends he eventually won his case against the *Daily Chronicle* but lost against *The Times*. Mangena stayed in London and alongside Isaac Pixley Seme was a consultant to the South African delegation to Britain to protest the Act of Union in 1909.

George Dixon Montsioa, was a student at the African Institute alongside D.D.T. Jabavu between 1903-1906. He studied law Lincoln's Inn in London and was called to the bar in 1910. He soon returned to Transvaal becoming only the third African barrister in South Africa. From Transvaal he moved to Johannesburg and became a founder member of the SANNC.

Sefako Mapogo Makgatho studied for three years in Ealing, London, arriving in 1882. Not much is known about his studies but upon returning to South Africa he established the Transvaal African Teachers Association, the

African National Political Union and was a founder member of the SANNC later becoming its vice-president.

The journeys, concerns, and activism of Msane, Montsioa, Makgatho, Mangena, and Seme reveal the Ethiopianist imperative in England. They came with a mission to study, to make like-minded contacts, to advocate on behalf of their homeland before returning there. They formed a Pan-African solidarity forged in British institutions. Though their primary focus was South Africa their scope was all Africans as demonstrated in the organisations they either set up or joined.

West Indian Students in Britain.

Many students from the West Indies brought an Ethiopianist activism to their stay in England. Probably the most famous during this period was Henry Sylvester Williams, whos' work I have already covered. Another example is John Quinlan of St. Lucia.

John Quinlan was a contributor to the Pan African Conference of 1900. He wrote a paper on *The Progress of Our People in Light of Current History*. Quinlan had been highlighting the plight of Africans in St. Lucia for many years. Little is known of his early life. He was registered as a 'Land Surveyor' in both St. Lucia and London which suggests he was well educated. In 1888, the 50th anniversary of the abolition of slavery, he organised a petition to Queen Victoria complaining of the state of freed Africans in St. Lucia. He also appeared before the West India Royal Commission in 1897. The Commission had been set up in response to complaints across the West Indies concerning the decline of the sugar industry, its consequences for workers and the lack of Government or Imperial assistance. He travelled to London in 1900 for the conference and stayed until 1903. Quinlan was an advocate of reparations and repatriation as demonstrated in his speeches at the conference.

> Sixty years ago, the Negroes of the West Indies were 'freed' - that is to say, cast without a penny and without a house, among hostile people and with no compensation for centuries of enforced labour. Why were the black men not given land on which to earn a living out of Crown Lands, sent back to their native Africa? Why were they left starving, houseless and helpless, at the mercy of their former owners? In spite of all, they had worked peacefully and made a subsistence for themselves and procured education for their children ...

Quinlan set out a clear strategy for reparations when addressing the Royal Commission.

> The Imperial Government ought to make a loan of 200,000 pounds Sterling in St. Lucia, not to bear interest until after ten years - the to bear one-and-a-half

percent interest, and three percent for a Sinking fund ... the Government should
establish four sugar factories in the Gros Islet district ...

Quinlan's argument echoed Ethiopianisms' call for reparations and
repatriation. He received no response from either local or Imperial authorities.

After addressing the P.A.C. he lived in London working as a Land Surveyor
where his activism continued. The Colonial Office, which had been watching
him, reported him as addressing meetings in Leeds and Bradford about the
need to "resuscitate the Sugar Industry in Saint Lucia". The Anti-Slavery
Reporter of March-May 1903 also reported on "his presence at meetings in
reference to forced labour".

Another key West Indian was Dr. Theophilus Scholes, a Jamaican born,
doctor and author who studied in Scotland and became a key member of the
British black activist movement. I will address him in the chapter on writers of
the Ethiopianist movement.

At the turn of the century Students were the vanguard of Ethiopianist
activism in Britain. They bore the responsibility to acquire skills, legal,
political, medicine, and science. They felt duty bound to carry out their
Ethiopianist imperative of education, organisation, dissemination, and
activism. Upon leaving England they continued to develop their Ethiopianist
inspired programs into liberation movements for African and Caribbean
independence. Movements in which they would assume important leadership
roles.

CHAPTER FOUR: THE LITERARY ETHIOPIANISTS

Britain has a long history of black activist literature from the 18th century with the abolitionist literature of Olaudah Equiano's *The Interesting Narrative of the Life of Olaudah Equiano* published in 1789. Ukawsaw Gronniosaw's *A Narrative of the Most Remarkable Particulars in the life of James Albert Ukawsaw Gronniosaw, an African Prince, as Related by Himself* published in 1772, Phillis Wheatley's *Poems on Various Subjects, Religious and Moral* published in 1773. This literature was predominantly biographical, bringing the experiences of enslaved Africans to a wider audience as part of the abolitionist movement during the end of the eighteenth and first half of the nineteenth century.

The Forerunners of Ethiopianist literature in Britain

By the beginning of the twentieth century Britain had become a centre of black literature and publishing with activists from around the world publishing their anti-colonial anti-imperial literature in the heart of the empire. The emergence of Ethiopianist literature in the U.S. earlier in the century had an impact beyond its shores. Two of the most influential Ethiopianist writers of the nineteenth century were David Walker who wrote *Appeal in Four Articles Together with A Preamble to the Coloured Citizens of the World* in 1829. And Edward Blyden's *Christianity, Islam, and the Negro Race* published in 1887. Both these books were circulated and discussed within black nationalist networks.

Edward Blyden in particular had a major impact on activists in Britain. He visited Britain many times where *Christianity, Islam and the Negro Race* was published in 1887. He travelled to Britain both in an official capacity as Liberian commissioner and as Liberian ambassador. He also travelled independently after he'd left his Liberia posts. He spoke at public meetings in Britain and met with a host of black activists. Some of his talks were published, *West Africa Before Europe and Other Addresses* published in 1905. *The Three Needs of Liberia* published in 1908, and *The Problems Before Liberia* published in 1909. In London 1903 he was guest of honour at a dinner given

Figure 36. Edward Blyden. Pioneer of Black Nationalism and regular visitor to Britain.

by 'West Africans residing in London' such was the esteem in which he was held. In his encouragement of ethnocentrism, he started from the premise that the Negro was endowed with special attributes, and that African customs and institutions represented a significant aspect of the character of the race. Blyden criticised foreign missionaries for seeking to Europeanize Africans and thus thwart the development of the 'African Personality'. He saw a compatibility with African customs and institutions and the highest tenets of Christianity. Blyden urged the setting up of an independent, non-denominational African

Church, and a secular West African University, controlled by Negroes themselves. He gained much support for these ideas from Native pastors. He founded a newspaper, *The Negro,* in April 1872 with the financial backing from five wealthy Natives. Upon leaving Liberia the newspaper was edited by Bishop James Johnson, Blyden's strongest ally among the Native pastors. Unfortunately, it was discontinued in 1874. Blyden helped found another newspaper the *West African Reporter* the declared aim of which was to "forge a bond of unity among English-speaking West Africans". From the 1870s he was writing articles in *Fraser's Magazine,* one of Britain's leading quarterlies. In 1872 he helped found the *The Ethiopian,* a monthly journal devoted to educational matters; through these outlets his views became common knowledge among literate West Africans. He would write articles for the *Lagos Weekly Record, The Sierra Leone Weekly News,* and *The Methodist Herald* in the 1890s. Blyden's vision of an independent African Church covering West Africa never fully came to light across the whole region, but smaller versions existed. In 1901 the United Native Church merged with the Independent Native Baptist Church founded by Majola Agbebi, a disciple of Blyden. J.C. Casely Hayford wrote of him:

> Edward W. Blyden has sought … to reveal everywhere the African to himself. He has been the voice of one crying in the wilderness of all these years calling upon all thinking Africans to go back to the rock from whence they were hewn by the common fathers of all nations. He further states Blyden "was a god descended upon earth to teach the Ethiopians anew the way of life.

Historian Holly Lynch writes that Blyden:

> was the most articulate and brilliant vindicator of black interests in the nineteenth century. His aim was to create among black people pride, confidence, and cultural identity" and he has been called "the most important historical progenitor of Pan-Africanism.

The last quote is important as it shows not just Blyden himself but the ideas of Ethiopianism as the progenitor of Pan-Africanism.

In his writings Blyden claimed that the African social system was naturally socialist, co-operative and equitable - an ideal for which Europe was desperately seeking as the answer to ills created by excessive individualism and unscrupulous competitiveness. Edward Blyden wrote thirteen books during his lifetime many of them published in London and held in the British museum. Blyden's vision of a West African superstate formed under colonialism but eventually controlled by Africans was visionary in its political, economic, and cultural projection of a post-colonial existence. His scientific approach to racism. His elevation of the special qualities of African people and

Figure 37. Dr Theophilus Scholes. Jamaican born medical student and Doctor in London. Prolific author of anti-colonial and anti-racist literature.

their glorious ancient heritage. His efforts to create an independent African church and independent African University embody Ethiopianist thinking perhaps more than any other author of the late nineteenth century.

British based Ethiopianist Writers

Late Victorian and early Edwardian black literature featured a range of topics and genres. Anti-colonial anti-racist literature, Novels, Autobiographies, Religious literature, and Scientific Research. A huge body of work, much of this literature expressed Ethiopianist ideas and their transition into Pan-Africanism. Publishing their works in London was an advantage for these writers. It meant their works would be disseminated throughout the black networks, across the diaspora, and in Africa itself. Likewise, these same networks would expose them to literature from Ethiopianists around the world.

A major Ethiopianist author from the Caribbean with strong links to the U.K. was Dr Theophilus Scholes. Jamaican born in 1858, he studied medicine in London and Edinburgh training to be a missionary physician. He spent five years in the Congo before returning to Britain where he established links with the African Institute in Colwyn Bay where he made links with other Ethiopianists like Pinley Isaka Seme. He travelled to Nigeria and returned to Britain in the late 1890s. He was a prolific author who wrote critical studies of British Imperialism and racism. His books also gave insight into the life of a black professional in Edwardian Britain. *The British Empire and Alliances: Britain's Duty to her Colonies and Subject Races* published in London 1899. In it he tells the story of a black doctor practicing medicine in a London hospital and the daily abuse he faces. Dr. Scholes expressed the view that colour prejudice was based on a delusion. *Glimpses of the Ages; Or, the 'Superior' and 'Inferior' Races, so-called, discussed in the light of Science and History.* Scholes was predicting "that war and revolution would be the motive force of social change in the future" published in 1905. Imanuel Geiss said of him (in his *The Pan-African Movement* 1974)

> Scholes belongs unmistakably in the twentieth century, for his arguments are quite modern; there is no further mention of the Bible. Although he scarcely ever identifies his sources, he must have been familiar with the preceding literature. After Blyden he was the first West Indian author to make an important contribution to the emergence of Pan-Africanism. Residing as he did in the capital city of the British Empire, he accepted the latter as a fact of life, and although critical of many details of colonial rule did not want to destroy it. His objective was to transform the Empire into a free association of equals of all men.

His book *Chamberlainism; his fiscal Proposals and Colonial Policy* published in London in 1903 under the pseudonym Bartholomew Smith. In it he criticizes the policies of Joseph Chamberlain for believing the empire was for settlement for white ignoring the black majority. He attacked Chamberlain's policies on protective Tariffs for white farmers, unequal pay between the races. Not just a writer he was a member of the African Society. He attended meetings at the house of commons keeping up to date on developments in Africa. He met regularly with Seme, Renner, Locke and other activists. He wrote a second volume of *Glimpses* 1908. His plan was for six volumes 'to inquire scientifically and historically into the circumstances in which the colourless people designate themselves the 'superior' and in which they designate the coloured races as 'inferior races'. Scholes (like Blyden) stated that Julius Caesar would never have believed that the people of England, that damp frontier of the glorious Roman Empire, would one day dominate

Figure 38. Reverend
Peter Thomas Stanford.
First African American
Pastor of an English
church. Ethiopianist
Author and public
speaker.

much of the globe". Scholes believed that the British would decline in the future - and that was as certain as her imperial rise had been unforeseen.

Scholes was born mid-nineteenth century which meant he was able to witness the gradual imposition of colonialism and the development of the racist ideology of Imperialism. A keen student of ancient empires and the works of black scholars Blyden and others Ethiopianist. He brought an analytical and historical perspective to his work which didn't involve the religious imperative of other Ethiopianists. His was a Pan-African perspective. His critical studies pre-empted later Pan-African critiques of colonialism and the ideology of racism. A very influential figure within the Edwardian black community. Due in part to his links with African, the Caribbean, and the U.S. He was sought out by the likes of Henry S. Williams, W.E. Dubois, and Arthur Schomberg. He died in London in 1940.

Contrast Scholes with the work of another writer in the Ethiopianist tradition based in Britain, Reverend Peter Thomas Stanford. Born into enslavement in the U.S. in 1859. Post enslavement he was baptised and joined anti-lynching organisations. He began writing articles, sermons, and essays on the subject. He became a Pastor in Canada. Efforts to raise funds for his church brought him to England in 1883. Settling in Birmingham he joined the SRBM. He became Pastor of the Hope Street Baptist Church in 1889, the first African American Pastor of an English church where he established himself as a public speaker of note and prolific author. He wrote *The Tragedy Of The Negro In America,* in three volumes beginning in 1897. Within it he describes the colonizing and Christianizing process of black communities and condemns the false Christianity imposed on blacks throughout the seventeenth and eighteenth centuries. He praises the works of Phyliss Wheatley and Frederick Douglass, as well as the growth of black schools and universities in the southern states of the U.S. In England he joined the Society for the Recognition of the Brotherhood of Man (SRBM) with Catherine Impey and spoke at many events. His best-known work was his autobiography *From Bondage To Liberty,* written in 1889. He charts his life journey, at times referring to himself as 'Mr Providence'. Firmly ensconced in the Ethiopianist ideas of a true Christianity, and the idea of self-upliftment through providence providing opportunity. His work on the history and condition of blacks in America does reveal a scientific approach. He returned to the U.S. in 1896.

Ethiopianist Writers published in Britain

An author who expressed his Ethiopianism through the relatively new genre of the historical novel was Ghanaian born J.C. Casely-Hayford. Already known as a giant of West African nationalism his novel *Ethiopia Unbound* published in 1911 is dedicated to "To the Sons of Ethiopia, The World Wide Over" Credited with being the first English language novel written by an African *Ethiopia Unbound* follows the journey of its main protagonist Kawmankra as he travels through England and Africa. He engages in philosophical and religious discourse with his white friend Silas. Through this discourse Casely Hayford asserts African cultures, traditions and religions as equal to that of Europeans. He links European culture to 'pagan' Roman culture. As Ugonna in his review states:

> The drift of Kwamankra's argument is that European philosophical, ethical and religious ideas were largely derived from Ethiopia, and Ethiopia ambiguously means Africa or Asia or both. By his logic Jesus Christ, Marcus Aurelius, Buddha, Confucious, Cleanthes and other stoics were Ethiopians since the idea of stoicism originated from Ethiopia.

In the Novel Whitely is shocked at the idea put forward by Kwamankra that "our Lord born of an Ethiopian woman". Kwamankra also challenges the

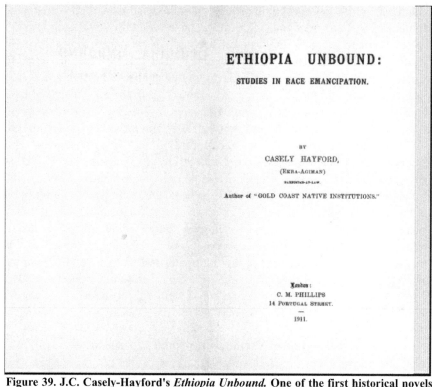

Figure 39. J.C. Casely-Hayford's *Ethiopia Unbound*. One of the first historical novels with an Ethiopianist theme published in Britain.

"feebleness of the idea of 'God' in the Anglo-Saxon language". He compares it to the corresponding word in Fanti 'Nyiakropon' which has a far more complex meaning and application. This radical reimagining of God in an African framework harks back to the origins of Ethiopianism. The character Kwamankra is clearly a mouthpiece for Casely Hayford's own ideas. He had long supported the idea of an African National University. In *Ethiopia Unbound* Kwamankra is a member of staff at an imagined National University.

> He was foremost in bringing forward schemes to prevent the work of the
> University becoming a mere foreign imitation ... no people who could despise
> its own language, customs, and institutions could hope to avoid national
> death... it was recognised that the best part of the teaching must be done in the
> people's own language, and soon several textbooks of authority had, with the
> kind permission of authors and publishers, been translated into Fanti, thereby
> making the progress of the student rapid and sound.

Publications such as Casely Hayford's own *Gold Coast Institutions* in 1903 John Mensah Sarbah's *Fanti Customary Laws* 1897 are examples of Africans studying and promoting their own culture. John Mensah Sarbah was a Ghanaian author educated in Britain. He qualified as a Barrister in 1897. He had articles published in the *Journal of the African Society* in 1904, and in Liverpool's *West African Mail* in 1905. An African historian who used ancient documentary sources and oral history. As a Barrister Sarbah looked after the interests of Ghanaian interest in land and taxation. In his work he was concerned to show that there existed "an African Social and Economic System most carefully and elaborately organized, venerable, impregnable, indispensable."

Other works of note written by Ethiopianist whilst in Britain include: S.J. Celestine Edwards *Hard Truth*. Salim Wilson *The Ethiopia Valley* published in 1906. Bandele Omoniyi *A Defence of the Ethiopian Movement* published in 1908. John Barbour-James *The Agricultural Possibilities* published in 1911.

Charters, Constitutions, Newspapers, and Journals

As well as in book form Ethiopianism had a strong role in formulizing and articulating what became the principles of Pan-Africanism in other forms of literature. The constitution of the Ethiopian Progressive Association launched in Liverpool 1904 in article II states;

> It shall be the object of this association: To create friendly feeling and intercourse among all its members; To create a bond of union between all members of the Ethiopian race at home and abroad; To further the interest and raise the social status of the Ethiopian race at home and abroad; To try to strengthen the friendly relationship between said race and the other races of mankind; To discuss at each meeting matters of vital importance concerning Africa in particular, and the Negro race in general.

If we compare this constitution with that of the written aims and objectives of later Pan African Congress', apart from differences in style of language used they are the same.

The many Ethiopianist black nationalist organisations already mentioned in previous chapters produced numerous Journals advocating black liberation. As has been already shown these were distributed in Britain and abroad.

London was also a hub for African newspapers. Predominantly West African, they were a means for activists in Britain to keep up to date with events in their homelands. Many activists based in London contributed articles to these publications. They included: *The African Telegraph, The Gold Coast, The Lagos Times, The West African Reporter, The Ethiopian, Lagos Weekly Record,* and *The Sierra Leone Weekly News.* These newspapers were vital in disseminating information to and mobilising the masses in Africa.

SUMMATION: THE ROLE OF ETHIOPIANISM IN THE PAN-AFRICAN MOVEMENT IN BRITAIN 1892-1906

The role of Ethiopianism was to enshrine in thought and deed the principles of global black nationalism. It was a unifying term. It meant wherever you were from you were part of a global African Liberation Movement. It was a major force in the creation of networks and organisations that would take these principles, formalised in the nineteenth century, into the twentieth century and beyond. Ethiopianism gave that movement a methodology that could be followed locally and internationally.

In Britain it was vital in providing an ideological and physical focus for black nationalists around the world to gather and collaborate. England was the place where a South African could meet a Trinidadian, an African American, a Nigerian, A Guyanese, and together they could form Associations which responded collectively to the needs of their homelands. It gave them a basis to create networks and organisations to facilitate their nationalist struggles. In doing so Ethiopianism played a significant role in making London a hub for black liberationists. Their experiences in Britain helped shape and transform their nationalist perspective into an internationalist one of supporting the struggles of their fellow Africans, an internationalist perspective that became known as Pan-Africanism. It facilitated African and Caribbean nations bringing their causes to the heart of the British empire. It gave a collective voice to and raised awareness of the plight of Africans at the height of colonial expansion and oppression.

As a spiritual movement it projected a viable alternative to the all-pervasive Eurocentric notions of spirituality and religious practice. Pan-African organisations since have followed suit in addressing the spiritual aspects of Black Liberation Theology and recognising the need for a spiritual solution that caters to the needs of Africans worldwide. Whether that be returning to traditional practices, creating new religions that fully embrace the Black experience, or using the currently dominant Abrahamic religions to advocate for Black liberation.

Ethiopianism was the first black movement to do these things on a global level, and London, England, was for a while its centre of global operations.

Ethiopianism - Its relevance today?

I am born and raised in Britain of Jamaican parentage. As well as detailing the Ethiopianist movement in Britain I also wanted to consider the relevance of my research in the context of todays' Black activism in Britain.

1.   The rise in diasporic Africans embracing African spiritual systems is a reflection not only of a growing awareness of indigenous practices, but of a rejection of Eurocentric Christianity and recognition of its key role in the oppression of Africans. However, as my research clearly shows African Christians were at the forefront of radical anti-colonial movements who promoted notions of a 'True Christianity'. For today's Black Christians this raises the question: What is the role of Black Liberation theology in Christian practice today?

2.   Ethiopianism facilitated an international exchange of Black students sharing ideas and information. They attended the highest European educational institutions but acted independently of these institutions, challenging them when necessary and organising themselves according to their independent needs. I believe there are lessons for todays' generation of students in both ideologies and methodologies practised by their student ancestors.

3.   In context of the Black Lives Matters movement and the 'Woke' generation in Britain. Ethiopianism needs to be given its proper place in the narrative of Black activism in the UK. The eighteenth and early nineteenth century abolitionists were Britain's first 'Woke' generation. Ethiopianism the second. The Black civil rights era of the 1960s and 70s the third. And todays' activists the fourth. The current generation needs to know the work of their activist ancestors in Britain. For example; the call for reparations, African-centred education, community economics, and pride in heritage. Black activists have been advocating for these in Britain for over one hundred and forty years.

4.   Ethiopianism is part of British history. The connections and collaborations between Ethiopianists and radical religious and workers groups in Britain had a profound impact on all involved. Therefore, Ethiopianism should be taught in the British education curriculum.

ABOUT THE AUTHOR

Danny Thompson

Author, Musician, Filmmaker, and Creator of Educational Products, Danny has been a music teacher for thirty years working in schools, colleges, and with organisations such as the London Philharmonic Orchestra.

As an independent filmmaker, he has written and directed dramas. He also composed soundtracks. In these capacities, he worked with Channel Four, BBC, BFI, and Sankofa films.

As a teacher of Black History and African Heritage, he devised and delivered educational projects and workshops for children and adults. He has worked with supplementary schools, community groups, and local authorities. He conducts tours of African artefacts in London museums and delivers online and in-person classes on Ethiopianism.

His work includes the educational Dvd: *Everyday Life in a West African Empire*. He wrote the book: T*he Afrikan Literary Heritage - History & Activities book*. He is also a co-creator of the online Black History adult education course: *The Black Secret,* which is at www.theblacksecret.co.uk.

In 2021 Danny attained his MRes in *African History and the History of the African Diaspora* from Chichester University.

To hire Danny Thompson as a guest speaker for your event, contact www.evolvingcreatives54@gmail

BIBLIOGRAPHY

Chapter One

Badra, Lahouel, *Ethiopianism and African Nationalism in South Africa before 1937* (Caheirs d'etudes Africaines Vol 26, 1986)

Casely-Hayford, J.E. *Ethiopia Unbound* (London: Frank Cass, 1911)

Barrett, Leonard, *The Rastafarian: Sounds of Cultural Dissonance* (Boston Beacon Press 1977)

Duncan, Graham, *Ethiopianism in Pan African Perspective 1880-1920* (Studia Historiae Ecclesiasticae Vol 41: 2015)

Esedebe, O, *Pan-Africanism: The idea and Movement 1776-1991* (Washington D.C: Howard University Press 1994)

Metafaria, Getachew, *The Ethiopian Connection to the Pan-African Movement* (University Press of Florida: 1995)

Price, Charles R. *Cleave to the Black: expressions of Ethiopianism in Jamaica* (New West Indian Guide, 2003)

Shepperson, George, *Ethiopianism and African Nationalism* (Clark Atlanta University, 1953)

Sundkler, Bengt, *Bantu Prophets in South Africa* (London OUP, 1948) Quoted in C.R. Price 'Cleave to the Black'

Walker, David, *Appeal in Four Articles* (University of North Carolina, Chapel Hill Library: 2011)

Chapter Two

Adi, H. *Pan-Africanism: A History* (London: Bloomsbury Publishing PLC 2018

Alexander, A.V, *Are South African Diamonds Worth their cost?* (Manchester: Labour Press 1897)

Allen, R. V, *Celestine Edwards; his life, work, and death* in *Lux* 2 Nov 1894

Bressey, C, *Race, Antiracism, and the Place of Blackness in the Making and Remaking of the English Working Class* (Historical Reflections, Vol 41, Issue 1) 2015

Celestine Edwards, S. J, *Christianity and Commerce,* in *Lux* 27 Aug. 1892

Celestine Edwards, S. J, *This World-ism,* in *Lux,* 3 Dec. 1892
Celestine Edwards, S. J, *Christianity and Progress,* in *Lux* 10 Sept
Celestine Edwards, S. J, *From Slavery To Bishopric* (London: John Kensit 1891)
Celestine Edwards, *The Negro Race and the British Protectorate,* in *Lux* 18 Feb 1893
Fraternity, 1st April 1896
Fraternity, 1st July 1896
Green, Jeffrey, *Black Edwardians, Black People in Britain 1901-1914* (Frank Cass, London, 1998)
Lorimer, D, *Legacies of slavery for race, religion, and empires* (Slavery & Abolition, 2018 Vol 39, No.4) The Guardian Newspaper, 9 Feb, 2006
Sherwood. M. *Origins of Pan-Africanism* (London: Routledge 2010)
John Simkin (john@spartacus-educational.com) Sept 1997
Daily Mail Newspaper, 19 Jun, 2020
Portsmouth Evening News, 14 August 1893, p. 2
The Friend, 22nd October 1897
Thomas, Theodore, *Hard Truth*
Williams, H. S. to Harriet Colenso, dd. (Gray's Inn, London, W.C. 9th June 1899)
The Lagos Times
The African Association Temple Papers, Lambeth Palace Library.
Mathurin, Williams (Hooker, Williams)

Chapter Three

Adi, H. *Bandele Omoniyi - A Neglected Nigerian Nationalist* (Oxford University Press 1991)
Bousquet, E. *Chronicle Of A Chronic Caribbean Chronicler* (St. Lucia News From The Voice 3rd August 2019)
Casely Hayford, J.E, *Ethiopia Unbound* (London: Frank Cass, 1911)
Collins, J, *Umuntu, ngumuntu, ngabuntu: the story of the African choir* (Studies in Theatre and Performance, 27. 2. 2007)
Fryer, Peter, *Staying Power* (London, Pluto Press 2018)
Harlan, Louis, *Washington: Black Leader* (Oxford University Press 1983)
Jabavu, D.D.T. *The Life of John Tengo Jabavu Editor of Imvo Zabantsundu 1884-1921* (Lovedale Institution Press 1922)
Killingray, David, *Significant Black South Africans in Britain before 1912* (South African Historical Journal, Vol 64, No.3 September2012)
Killingray, David & Edwards, Joel, *Black Voices: The Shaping of our Christian Experience* (England: Inter Varsity Press 2007)

Mitchell, Henry. *When the world came to Scotland; student radicals at Edinburgh University 1906-46* (Scottish Critical Heritage) 2018

Omoniyi, B, *A Defense of the Ethiopian Movement* (Edinburgh, 1908

Shephard, B. *Kitty and the Prince* (London: Profile Books 2007)

Sherwood, M. *Activists, Visionaries, Artists; Chapter 5; Two Pan-African Political Activists Emanating from Edinburgh University* (Koninkluke Brill, NY, Leiden 2004)

Irish Times 15 March 1892

Christian Express, August 1892

Stead, W. *The Review of Reviews* (September 1891)

Lagos Standard 1906

South Africa (September 1892)

Chapter Four

Casely, Hayford, J.C, *Ethiopia Unbound* (London: C.M. Phillips 1911)

Blyden, E. W, *African Life and Customs* (London, 1908)

Blyden, E.W. *West Africa Before Europe* introduction

Blyden, E. *Christianity, Islam and the Negro Race* (London: Createspace)

Fryer, P. *Staying Power* (London: Pluto Press 2018

Geiss, I, *The Pan-African Movement* (London: Rex Collins 1975)

Green, J. *Black Edwardians* (London: Frank Cass 1009)

Holden, E, *Blyden of Liberia* (New York: Vantage, 1966)

Lynch, J, *Edward Wilmot Blyden: Pan-African Patriot 1832-1912* (Oxford University Press 1967)

Lynch, H. *Edward W. Blyden: Pioneer West African Nationalist* (London: Cambridge University Press - *The Journal of African History,* Vol 6, No. 3 1965)

T. Scholes, T. *Glimpses of the Ages - Vol 2* (London: John Long 1903)

Stanford, P. *The Tragedy of The Negro In America* (www.docsouth.unc.edu)

Stanford, P. *From Bondage To Liberty* (England: Smethwick 1889)

Non-Referenced Bibliography

Crockett, Hasan, *The Incendiary Pamphlet: David Walker's Appeal in Georgia* (University of Chicago Press on behalf of the Association for the Study of African American Life and History 2001)

Giess, I, *Notes on The Development of Pan-Africanism* (Historical Society of Nigeria 1967)

Jenkins, R, *Gold Coasters Overseas 1880-1919* (Taylor and Francis 2010)

Killingray, David, *Rights, Land, and Labour: Black British Critics of South African Policies before 1948* (Taylor and Francis 2009)

Moses, Wilson, J, *The Golden Age of Black Nationalism 1850-1925; Ch. 8 - The Poetics of Ethiopianism* (Oxford University Press 1988)

Nwauva, Apollos, *Far Ahead of His Time: James Africanus Horton's Initiatives for a West African University and His Frustrations, 1862 - 1871* (Cahiers d,Etudes Africanes, 1999, Vol. 39, pp. 107-121)

Osei-Nyame, Kwadwo, *Pan-Africanist Ideology and the African Historical Novel of Self -Discovery* (Taylor & Francis 1999)

Scott, William, *The Ethiopian Ethos in African American Thought* (Tsehai Publishers 2004)

Wahle, Kathleen, O'Mara *Alexander Crummell: Black Evangelist and Pan-Negro Nationalist* (Clark Atlanta University 1968)

INDEX

Printed in Great Britain
by Amazon

30775541R00056